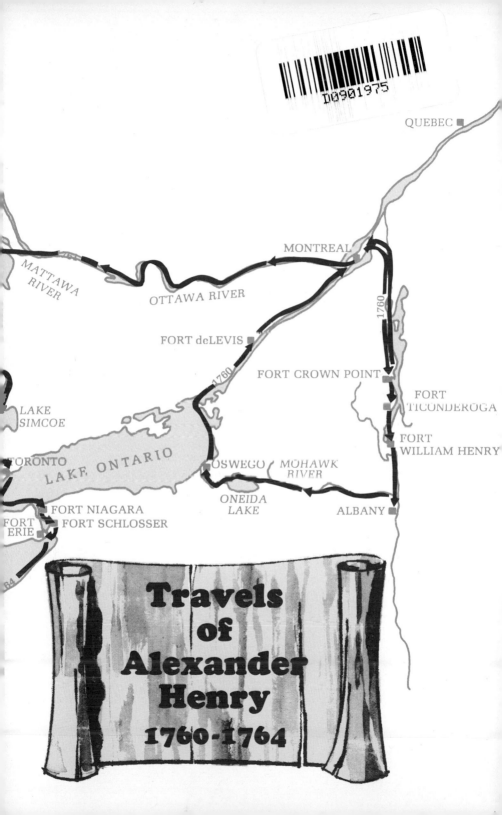

QUEBEC ■

MONTREAL

MATTAWA
RIVER

OTTAWA RIVER

1760

FORT deLEVIS ■

1760

FORT CROWN POINT ■

FORT
TICONDEROGA

LAKE
SIMCOE

FORT
WILLIAM HENRY

TORONTO

LAKE ONTARIO

OSWEGO   MOHAWK
RIVER

ONEIDA
LAKE

ALBANY ■

FORT NIAGARA
FORT
ERIE   FORT SCHLOSSER

R4

Travels
of
Alexander
Henry
1760-1764

TRAVELS

AND ADVENTURES

IN

CANADA

AND

THE INDIAN TERRITORIES,

BETWEEN

THE YEARS 1760 AND 1776.

IN TWO PARTS.

BY ALEXANDER HENRY, ESQ.

NEW-YORK:

PRINTED AND PUBLISHED BY I. RILEY.

....

1809.

ATTACK
AT
MICHILIMACKINAC

Alexander Henry's
Travels and Adventures in
Canada and the Indian Territories
between the years
1760 and 1764

Edited by

David A. Armour

Illustrated by

Dirk Gringhuis

Mackinac Island State Park Commission
Mackinac Island, Michigan

Copyright 1971   15,000 copies
Standard Book Number 911872-31-0
Printed by TriKraft, Inc.

TO

THE RIGHT HONOURABLE

SIR JOSEPH BANKS, BARONET ;

KNIGHT COMPANION

OF THE MOST HONOURABLE ORDER OF THE BATH ;

ONE OF HIS MAJESTY'S

MOST HONOURABLE PRIVY COUNCIL ;

PRESIDENT OF THE ROYAL SOCIETY, F. S. A.

&c. &c. &c.

THIS VOLUME

WITH GREAT DEFERENCE,

IS MOST RESPECTFULLY DEDICATED,

BY

HIS VERY DEVOTED,

AND VERY HUMBLE SERVANT,

ALEXANDER HENRY.

Montreal, October 20th, 1809.

CONTENTS

PREFACE.

A PREMATURE attempt to share in the fur-trade of Canada, directly on the conquest of the country, led the author of the following pages into situations of some danger and singularity ; and the pursuit, under better auspices, of the same branch of commerce, occasioned him to visit various parts of the Indian Territories.

These transactions occupied a period of sixteen years, commencing nearly with the author's setting out in life. The details, from time to time committed to paper, form the subject matter of the present volume.

The heads, under which, for the most part, they will be found to range themselves, are three: first, the incidents or adventures in which the author was engaged; secondly, the observations, on the geography and natural history of the countries visited, which he was able to make, and to preserve;

and, thirdly, the views of society and manners, among a part of the Indians of North America, which it has belonged to the course of his narrative to develope.

Upon the last, the author may be permitted to remark, that he has by no means undertaken to write the general history of the American Indians, nor any theory of their morals, or their merits. With but few exceptions, it has been the entire scope of his design, simply to relate those particular facts, which are either identified with his own fortunes, or with the truth of which he is otherwise personally conversant. All comment, therefore, in almost all instances, is studiously avoided.

MONTREAL, October 20th, 1809.

ILLUSTRATIONS

INTRODUCTION

An old man sat hunched over a writing table scribbling furiously with a scratchy quill pen. Memories of bygone days flashed through his mind as he sought to transfer them to the paper in front of him before old age obliterated them completely. Despite his seventy years Alexander Henry still clearly recalled the day over forty-five years before when he had crouched in a darkened attic in Michilimackinac while painted Indians in the room below shrieked for his blood. Some of the details were blurred, but the basic outline remained crystal clear. As he wrote, Henry could almost smell the bear grease on the sweating Indians who led him away into the wilderness a dejected captive. Henry wanted to recapture the spirit and excitement of a bygone era, for in 1809, when he wrote, only a few of the original English traders who had first penetrated the Great Lakes country after it was seized from the French in 1760 still survived.

Though he recalled his boyhood in New Jersey, where he had been born in 1739, Henry decided to begin his narrative in 1760, when as a young man of twenty-one he set off to exploit the numerous possibilities which life afforded. Henry grew up during the stirring years of the French and Indian War, when France and Great Britain strove mightily for ultimate domination of the riches of North America. The war which began in 1754 with the defeat of the young Virginian, George Washington, in a wilderness glen of western Pennsylvania had at first gone badly against the English. The ignominious defeat of General Braddock was followed in sickening succession by the fall of Forts Oswego and William Henry on the frontiers of New York.

Eventually realizing the importance of capturing Canada, the English Parliament despatched thousands of troops to North America and turned the tide. Finally in 1759 General James Wolfe's redcoated regulars scaled the cliffs of Quebec and decisively defeated the French on the Plains of Abraham. Meanwhile a large force led by Jeffery Amherst secured the capitulation of Forts Ticonderoga and Crown Point on Lake Champlain.

In the following year the British closed a gigantic pinchers against Montreal, the capital of French Canada, by sending one force up the Saint Lawrence while Amherst led his troops in a roundabout way from Albany, New York up the Mohawk River to Lake Ontario and then eastward down the Saint Lawrence River. Alexander Henry accompanied Amherst's forces as a private trader, intent on making his fortune selling supplies to the troops. Having purchased a stock of merchandise in Albany, he followed the soldiers to Lake Ontario, where for the first time he beheld the vast water network which was to shape his future. Within a few months, on September 8, 1760, Montreal surrendered, and the economic pattern of the vast Great Lakes region was revolutionized. Formerly closed to British traders, these rich beaver lands were now open to anyone with the courage and persistence to penetrate the hostile interior. Alexander Henry was such a man.

Though the French had surrendered, their Indian allies, having suffered no defeat, viewed with hatred and suspicion the Englishman who dared appear in their country. Indian hostility dominates Henry's account, and the likelihood of sudden death imparts a tension and drama which the reader will not soon forget. Disgruntled by their betrayal by the French, dissatisfied by the lack of presents from the English, alarmed by the British restriction on selling them gunpowder, and unified by the messianic message of the Delaware Prophet, the smoldering Indian discontent needed only the spark of Pontiac's attack on Detroit to set the entire Northwest frontier ablaze. Henry himself was caught up in the brutal Chippewa attack on Fort Michilimackinac, Michigan and his narrative is famous as the most detailed account of that grisly incident. Contemporary documents written by others who witnessed the butchery on that fatal Thursday, June 2, 1763 attest to the main details of Henry's recollection. Sometimes, however, bitter emotions clouded his judgment, and his hostile assessment of the Frenchman Charles Langlade, Jr. is not born out by Captain George Etherington, commander of the fort, who paid high tribute to Langlade for his role in preserving both the men and merchandise in Michilimackinac during and after the attack.

Henry's account of his canoe voyage to Michilimackinac and his subsequent journey as a captive paints a rich panorama of life, both Indian and White, on the upper Great Lakes from 1760-1764. All of the three major routes into the interior, the Ottawa River-Lake Nipissing route, the Lake Simcoe-Georgian Bay route and the Lake Erie-Detroit route, were traversed and their dangers and beauties described. Excursions were also made to Sault Sainte Marie and the eastern shore of Lake Michigan, but the spot to which Henry repeatedly returns is Michilimackinac, the major trade entrepot in the upper Great Lakes. The centrality of Michilimackinac to the fur trade of the 1760's is emphasized again and again.

Henry gives a vivid picture of life at the stockaded fort at Michilimackinac in the crucial period of transition from French to English control and during the uncertain interlude of Indian supremacy in 1763 and 1764. Forced to live as an Indian captive for over a year, Henry also became intimately acquainted with the Indian's mode of living, praying and dying and affords the reader a unique insight into the Indian culture which supported the post at Michilimackinac with food and furs.

Henry's entire account is nearly twice as long as reprinted here and carries the story to 1776. Henry himself divided his book into two parts and we have reprinted only Part One. Part Two deals primarily with Henry's journeys to Lake Superior and far beyond into the Canadian Northwest. For those wishing to read the entire account three editions are available. The first is the rare original edition published in New York in 1809. A scholarly facsimile reprint edited by James Bain appeared in 1901, and the last complete edition was annotated in 1921 by Milo Quaife for Lakeside Press, Chicago.*

In the present edition the editor has retained Henry's text and footnotes while deleting his lengthy chapter titles and inserting the editor's own. Punctuation and occasionally spelling have also been modernized. Editorial comments enclosed in brackets have been inserted in the text, and on occasion the author's notes have been moved to the body of the text.

Enough has been said of the importance of Henry's narrative. It is now time for the editor to stand aside and let the grizzled old fur trader tell his own tale.

David A. Armour

Milwaukee, Wisconsin
January 31, 1966

---

*In 1969 the Charles E. Tuttle Company at Rutland, Vermont reprinted the Bain edition with a new introduction by L. G. Thomas.

Portrait of Alexander Henry

1

THE MAKING
of A
FUR TRADER

In the year 1760, when the British arms under General Amherst were employed in the reduction of Canada, I accompanied the expedition which subsequently to the surrender of Quebec *(Quebec surrendered on the eighteenth of September, 1759.-Author)* descended from Oswego on Lake Ontario against Fort de Levi, one of the upper posts situate on an island which lies on the south side of the great river St. Lawrence, at a short distance below the mouth of the Oswegatchie.* Fort de Levi surrendered on the twenty-first day of August, seven days after the commencement of the siege; and General Amherst continued his voyage down the stream, carrying his forces against Montreal.

It happened that in this voyage one of the few fatal accidents which are remembered to have occurred in that dangerous part of the river below Lake St. Français, called the Rapides des Cédres, befell the British army. Several boats loaded with provisions and military stores were lost, together with upward of a hundred men. I had three boats loaded with merchandise, all of which were lost; and I saved my life only by gaining the bottom of one of my boats, which lay among the rocky shelves, and on which I continued for some hours, and until I was kindly taken off by one of the General's aides-de-camp.

The surrender of Montreal, and with it the surrender of all Canada, followed that of Fort de Levi at only the short interval of three days, and proposing to avail myself of the new market which was thus thrown open to British adventure, I hastened to Albany, where my commercial connections were, and where I procured a quantity of goods with which I set out, intending to carry them to Montreal. For this, however, the winter was too near approached; I was able only to return to Fort de Levi (to

*Now Ogdensburgh, N. Y. - Editor.

1

which the conquerors had now given the name of Fort William Augustus) and where I remained until the month of January in the following year.

At this time, having disposed of my goods to the garrison and the season for traveling on the snow and ice being set in, I prepared to go down to Montreal. The journey was to be performed through a country inhabited only by Indians and by beasts of the forest, and which presented to the eye no other change than from thick woods to the broad surface of a frozen river. It was necessary that I should be accompanied as well by an interpreter as by a guide, to both of which ends I engaged the services of a Canadian, named Jean Baptiste Bodoine.

The snow which lay upon the ground was by this time three feet in depth. The hour of departure arriving, I left the fort on snowshoes, an article of equipment which I had never used before, and which I found it not a little difficult to manage. I did not avoid frequent falls; and when down I was scarcely able to rise.

At sunset on the first day we reached an Indian encampment of six lodges and about twenty men. As these people had been very recently employed offensively against the English, in the French service, I agreed but reluctantly to the proposal of my guide and interpreter, which was nothing less than that we should pass the night with them. My fears were somewhat lulled by his information that he was personally acquainted with those who composed the camp, and by his assurances that no danger was to be apprehended; and being greatly fatigued, I entered one of the lodges, where I presently fell asleep.

Unfortunately Bodoine had brought upon his back a small keg of rum, which, while I slept, he opened, not only for himself but for the general gratification of his friends; a circumstance of which I was first made aware in being awakened by a kick on the breast from the foot of one of my hosts, and by a yell or Indian cry which immediately succeeded. At the instant of opening my eyes I saw that my assailant was struggling with one of his companions, who, in conjunction with several women, was endeavoring to restrain his ferocity. Perceiving, however, in the countenance of my enemy the most determined mischief, I sprung upon my feet, receiving in so doing a wound in my hand from a knife which had been raised to give a more serious wound. While the rest of my guardians continued their charitable efforts for my protection, an old woman took hold of my arm, and making signs that I should accompany her, led me out of the lodge, and then gave me to understand that unless I fled or could conceal myself I should certainly be killed.

My guide was absent, and without his direction I was at a loss where to go. In all the surrounding lodges there was the same howling and violence as in that from which I had escaped. I was without my snowshoes, and had only so much clothing as I had fortunately left upon me when I lay down to sleep. It was now one o'clock in the morning in the month of January, and in a climate of extreme rigor.

I was unable to address a single word in her own language to the old woman who had thus befriended me; but on repeating the name of Bodoine, I soon found that she comprehended my meaning; and having first pointed to a large tree, behind which she made signs that until she could find my guide I should hide myself, she left me on this important errand. Meanwhile, I made my way to the tree and seated myself in the snow. From my retreat I beheld several Indians running from one lodge to another, as if to quell the disturbance which prevailed.

The coldness of the atmosphere congealed the blood about my wound and prevented further bleeding; and the anxious state of my mind rendered me almost insensible to bodily suffering. At the end of half an hour I heard myself called by Bodoine, whom, on going to him, I found as much intoxicated and as much a savage as the Indians themselves; but he was nevertheless, able to fetch my snowshoes from the lodge in which I had left them, and to point out to me a beaten path, which presently entered a deep wood, and which he told me I must follow.

After walking about three miles I heard, at length, the footsteps of my guide, who had now overtaken me. I thought it most prudent to abstain from all reproof; and we proceeded on our march till sunrise, when we arrived at a solitary Indian hunting lodge, built with branches of trees, and of which the only inhabitants were an Indian and his wife. Here the warmth of a large fire reconciled me to a second experiment on Indian hospitality. The result was very different from that of the one which had preceded it; for after relieving my thirst with melted snow and my hunger with a plentiful meal of venison, of which there was a great quantity in the lodge, and which was liberally set before me, I resumed my journey, full of sentiments of gratitude, such as almost obliterated the recollection of what had befallen me among the friends of my benefactors.

From the hunting lodge I followed my guide till evening, when we encamped on the banks of the St. Lawrence, making a fire and supping on the meat with which our wallets had been filled in the morning.

While I indulged myself in rest my guide visited the shore, where he discovered a bark canoe which had been left there in the beginning of the winter by some Indian wayfarers. We were now at the head of the Longue Sault, one of those portions of the river in which it passes over a shallow, inclining, and rocky bed, and where its motion consequently prevents it from freezing, even in the coldest part of the year; and my guide, as soon as he had made his discovery, recommended that we should go by water down the rapids, as the means of saving time, of shortening our journey, and of avoiding a numerous body of Indians then hunting on the banks below. The last of these arguments was with me so powerful that though a bark canoe was a vehicle to which I was altogether a stranger, though this was a very small one of only sixteen or eighteen feet in length* and much out of repair, and though the misfortune which I had experienced in the navigation of these rocky parts of the St. Lawrence when descending with the army naturally presented itself to my mind as a still further discouragement, yet I was not long in resolving to undertake the voyage.

Accordingly, after stopping the leaks as completely as we were able, we embarked and proceeded. My fears were not lessened by perceiving that the least unskillful motion was sufficient to overset the ticklish craft into which I had ventured; by the reflection that a shock comparatively gently from a mass of rock or ice was more than its frail material could sustain; nor by observing that the ice, which lined the shores of the river, was too strong to be pushed through and at the same time too weak to be walked upon, so that in the event of disaster it would be almost impossible to reach the land. In fact, we had not proceeded more than a mile when our canoe became full of water, and it was not till after a long search that we found a place of safety.

Treading once more upon dry ground, I should willingly have faced the wilderness and all its Indians rather than embark again; but my guide informed me that I was upon an island, and I had therefore no choice before me. We stopped the leaks a second time and recommenced our voyage, which we performed with success, but sitting all the way in six inches of water. In this manner we arrived at the foot of the rapids, where the river was frozen all across. Here we disembarked upon the ice, walked to the bank, made a fire, and *encamped*; for such is the phrase employed in the woods of Canada.

At daybreak the next morning we put on our snowshoes and commenced our journey over the ice; and at ten o'clock arrived in sight of Lake St. Francais, which is from four to six miles in breadth. The wind was high and the snow, drifting over the expanse, prevented us at times from discovering the land, and consequently (for compass we had none) from pursuing with certainty our course.

---

*There are still smaller. -Author.

4

Toward noon the storm became so violent that we directed our steps to the shore on the north side by the shortest route we could; and making a fire, dined on the remains of the Indian hunter's bounty. At two o'clock in the afternoon, when the wind had subsided and the atmosphere grown more clear, I discerned a *cariole*, or sledge, moving our way, and immediately sent my guide to the driver with a request that he would come to my encampment. On his arrival I agreed with him to carry me to Les Cédres, a distance of eight leagues, for a reward of eight dollars. The driver was a Canadian who had been to the Indian village of St. Regis and was now on his return to Les Cédres, then the uppermost white settlement on the St. Lawrence.

Late in the evening I reached Les Cédres and was carried to the house of M. Leduc, its seignior, by whom I was politely and hospitably received. M. Leduc being disposed to converse with me, it became a subject of regret that neither party understood the language of the other; but an interpreter was fortunately found in the person of a sergeant of His Majesty's Eighteenth Regiment of Foot.

I now learned that M. Leduc in the earlier part of his life had been engaged in the fur trade with the Indians of Michili- mackinac and Lake Superior. He informed me of his acquaintance with the Indian languages and his knowledge of furs, and gave me to understand that Michilimackinac was richer in this com- modity than any other part of the world. He added that the Indians were a peaceable race of men, and that an European might travel from one side of the continent to the other without experiencing insult. Further, he mentioned that a *guide* who lived at no great distance from his house could confirm the truth of all that he had advanced.

I, who had previously thought of visiting Michilimackinac with a view of the Indian trade, gave the strictest attention to all that fell on this subject from my host; and in order to possess myself as far as possible of all that might be collected in addition, I requested that the *guide* should be sent for. This man arrived, and a short conversation terminated in my engaging him to con- duct myself, and the canoes which I was to procure, to Michili- mackinac in the month of June following.

There being at this time no goods in Montreal adapted to the Indian trade, my next business was to proceed to Albany to make my purchases there. This I did in the beginning of the month of May, by the way of Lake Champlain; and on the fifteenth of June arrived again in Montreal, bringing with me my outfits. As I was altogether a stranger to the commerce in which I was engaging, I confided in the recommendations given me of one Etienne Campion, as my assistant; a part which he uniformly fulfilled with honesty and fidelity.

His Excellency, General [Thomas] Gage, who now commanded in chief in Canada, very reluctantly granted me the permission at this time requisite for going to Michilimackinac. No treaty of peace had yet been made between the English and the Indians, which latter were in arms under Pontiac, an Indian leader of more than common celebrity, and General Gage was therefore strongly and (as it became manifest) but too justly apprehensive that both the property and lives of His Majesty's subjects would be very insecure in the Indian countries. But he had already granted such permission to a Mr. [Henry] Bostwick, and this I was able to employ as an argument against his refusal in respect to myself. General Gage complied, and on the third day of August, 1761, after some further delay in obtaining a passport from the town-major, I dispatched my canoes to Lachine, there to take in their lading.

Thirty-five foot long birch bark canoe on display at Fort Michilimackinac

2

BY CANOE
from MONTREAL
to MICHILIMACKINAC

The inland navigation from Montreal to Michilimackinac may be performed either by the way of Lakes Ontario and Erie, or by the river Des Outaouais, [Ottawa River], Lake Nipisingue, [Lake Nipissing], and the river Des Français, [French River], for as well by one as the other of these routes we are carried to Lake Huron. The second is the shortest and that which is usually pursued by the canoes employed in the Indian trade.

The canoes which I provided for my undertaking were, as is usual, five fathoms and a half in length and four feet and a half in their extreme breadth, and formed of birch-tree bark a quarter of an inch in thickness. The bark is lined with small splints of cedar-wood; and the vessel is further strengthened with ribs of the same wood, of which the two ends are fastened to the gunwales; several bars, rather than seats, are also laid across the canoe, from gunwale to gunwale. The small roots of the spruce tree afford the wattap, with which the bark is sewed; and the gum of the pine tree supplies the place of tar and oakum. Bark, some spare wattap, and gum are always carried in each canoe for the repairs which frequently become necessary.

The canoes are worked, not with oars but with paddles, and occasionally with a sail. To each canoe there are eight men; and to every three or four canoes, which constitute a *brigade*, there is a *guide* or conductor. Skilful men, at double the wages of the rest, are placed in the head and stern. They engage to go from Montreal to Michilimackinac and back to Montreal again, the middle-men at one hundred and fifty livres [twenty-five dollars] and the end men at three hundred livres [fifty dollars]* each. The *guide* has the command of his brigade and is answerable for all

---

*These particulars may be compared with those of a more modern date, given in the *Voyages* of Sir Alexander Mackenzie. -Author.

pillage and loss; and in return every man's wages is answerable to him. This regulation was established under the French government.

The freight of a canoe of the substance and dimensions which I have detailed consists in sixty *pieces*, or packages of merchandise, of the weight of from ninety to a hundred pounds each, and provisions to the amount of one thousand weight. To this is to be added the weight of eight men and of eight bags weighing forty pounds each, one of which every man is privileged to put on board. The whole weight must therefore exceed eight thousand pounds, or may perhaps be averaged at four tons.

The nature of the navigation which is to be described will sufficiently explain why the canoe is the only vessel which can be employed along its course. The necessity, indeed, becomes apparent at the very instant of our departure from Montreal itself.

The St. Lawrence for several miles immediately above Montreal descends with a rapid current over a shallow, rocky bed; insomuch that even canoes themselves, when loaded, cannot resist the stream, and are therefore sent empty to Lachine, where they meet the merchandise which they are to carry, and which is transported thither by land.* Lachine is about nine miles higher up the river than Montreal, and is at the head of the Sault de St. Louis, which is the highest of the *saults*, falls, or *leaps* in this part of the St. Lawrence.

On the third of August I sent my canoes to Lachine, and on the following morning embarked with them for Michilimackinac. The river is here so broad as to be denominated a lake, by the title of Lake St. Louis; the prospect is wide and cheerful; and the village has several well-built houses.

In a short time we reached the rapids and carrying-place of St. Anne, two miles below the upper end of the island of Montreal; and it is not till after passing these that the voyage may be properly said to be commenced. At St. Anne's the men go to confession, and at the same time offer up their vows; for the saint from whom this parish derives its name and to whom its church is dedicated, is the patroness of the Canadians in all their travels by water.**

There is still a further custom to be observed on arriving at St. Anne's, and which is that of distributing eight gallons of rum to each canoe (a gallon for each man) for consumption during the voyage; nor is it less according to custom to drink the whole

---

*La Chine, or China, has always been the point of departure for the upper countries. It owes its name to the expeditions of M. de la Salle which were fitted out at this place for the discovery of a northwest passage to China. -Author.

**Ste. Anne de Michilimackinac is so named for the same reason. -Editor.

of this liquor upon the spot. The saint, therefore, and the priest were no sooner dismissed than a scene of intoxication began in which my men surpassed, if possible, the drunken Indian in singing, fighting, and the display of savage gesture and conceit. In the morning we reloaded the canoes and pursued our course across the Lake des Deux Montagnes.

This lake, like that of St. Louis, is only a part of the estuary of the Outaouais, which here unites itself with the St. Lawrence, or rather, according to some, the Cataraqui; for, with these, the St. Lawrence is formed by the confluence of the Cataraqui and Outaouais.*

At noon we reached the Indian Mission of the Seminary of St. Sulpice, situate on the north bank of the lake, with its two villages, Algonquin and Iroquois, in each of which was reckoned an hundred souls. Here we received a hospitable reception and remained during two hours. I was informed by one of the missionaries that since the conquest of the country the unrestrained introduction of spirituous liquors at this place, which had not been allowed under the former government, had occasioned many outrages.

At two o'clock in the afternoon we prosecuted our voyage; and at sunset disembarked and encamped at the foot of the *Longue Sault*. There is a Longue Sault both on this river and on the St. Lawrence.

At ten leagues [thirty miles] above the island of Montreal I passed the limits of the cultivated lands on the north bank of the Outaouais. On the south, the farms are very few in number, but the soil has every appearance of fertility.**

In ascending the Longue Sault, a distance of three miles, my canoes were three times unladen, and together with their freight carried on the shoulders of the *voyageurs*. The rocky carrying-places are not crossed without danger of serious accidents by men bearing heavy burdens.

The Longue Sault being passed, the Outaouais presented on either side only scenes of primitive forest, the common range of the deer, the wolf, the bear, and the Indian. The current is here gentle. The lands upon the south are low, and when I passed them were overflowed; but on the northern side the banks are dry and elevated, with much meadow land at their feet. The grass in some places was high. Several islands are in this part of the river. Among the fish, of which there are abundance, are catfish of a large size.

*This is the *Utawas* of some writers, the *Ottaway* of others, etc., etc., etc. It is also called the Grand River —*la Grande Rivière*. -Author.

**Numerous and thriving colonists are now enjoying that fertility— 1809. -Author.

9

At fourteen leagues above the Longue Sault we reached a French fort, or trading house, surrounded by a stockade. Attached was a small garden from which we procured some vegetables. The house had no inhabitant. At three leagues farther is the mouth of the Hare River, which descends from the north, and here we passed another trading house. At a few leagues still higher on the south bank is the mouth of a river four hundred yards wide, and which falls into the Outaouais perpendicularly from the edge of a rock forty feet high. The appearance of this fall has procured for it the name of the *rideau*, or *curtain*; and hence the river itself is called the Rideau, or *Rivière du Rideau*. The fall presented itself to my view with extraordinary beauty and magnificence, and decorated with a variety of colors.

Still ascending the Outaouais, at three leagues from the fall of the Rideau is that of La Grande Chaudière, *(the Great Kettle -Author)*, a phenomenon of a different aspect. Here, on the north side of the river, is a deep chasm running across the channel for about two hundred yards, from twenty-five to thirty feet in depth and without apparent outlet. In this receptacle a large portion of the river falls perpendicularly with a loud noise, and amid a cloud of spray and vapor, but embellished from time to time with the bright and gorgeous rainbow. The river at this place is a mile in width. In the rainy season the depth of the fall is lessened by reason of the large quantity of water which is received into the chasm, and which for want, as it would seem, of a sufficient drain, in part, fills it up. At such times an eddy and an accumulation of foam at a particular part of the chasm have led me to suspect the existence of an opening beneath through which the water finds a subterranean passage. The rock which forms the bed of the river appears to be split in an oblique direction from one shore to the other; and the chasm on the north side is only a more perfect breach.

The fall of La Grande Chaudière is more than twenty leagues above the Longue Sault. Its name is justified both by its form and by the vapor, or steam, which ascends from it. Above it there are several islands, of which the land is higher at the upper than at the lower extremities. The carrying-place is not more than a quarter of a mile in length, over a smooth rock, and so near the fall that the men in passing are wetted by the spray. From this carrying-place to another of rather more length, called the Portage de la Chaudière and sometimes the Second Chaudière, is only three miles.

In this part of the voyage I narrowly escaped a fatal accident. A thunder-gust having obliged us to make the shore, the men went into the woods for shelter while I remained in my canoe under a covering of bark. The canoe had been intended to be sufficiently drawn aground; but to my consternation it was not long before, while thus left alone, I perceived it to be adrift and going with the current toward La Grande Chaudière. Happily I made a timely discovery of my situation, and getting out in shallow water was enabled by the assistance of the men, who soon heard my call, to save my property along with my life.

At twelve miles from the second Portage de la Chaudière there is a third Chaudière, but also called the Portage des Chenes. The name of the carrying-place is derived from the oak trees with which it abounds. It is half a mile in length, level, and of an agreeable aspect.

The bed of the river is here very broad for a space of twelve leagues, or thirty-six miles; and in this part of its course it is called Lake des Chaudières, a name derived from the falls below. The current, in this place, is scarcely perceptible. The lands, on either side are high, and the soil is good. At the head of Lake des Chaudières, is the Portage des Châts. The carrying-place is a high, uneven rock of difficult access. The ridge of rock crosses the stream and occasions not only one but numerous falls, separated from each other by islands and affording a scene of very pleasing appearance. At the distance of a mile seven openings present themselves to the eye along a line of two miles, which at this point is the breadth of the river. At each opening is a fall of water of about thirty feet in height, and which from the whiteness of its foam might be mistaken for a snowbank. Above, for six miles there are many islands, between which the current is strong. To overcome the difficulties of this part of the navigation the canoes first carry one-half of their loading, and at a second trip the remainder.

Above the islands the river is six miles in width, and is called Lake des Châts. The lake, so called, is thirty miles long. The lands about the lake are like those of Lake des Chaudières; but higher up they are both high and rocky, and covered with no other wood than spruce and stunted pine.

While paddling against the gentle current of Lake des Châts we met several canoes of Indians returning from their winter's hunt to their village at the Lake des Deux Montagnes. I purchased some of their maple sugar and beaver skins in exchange for provisions. They wished for rum, which I declined to sell them; but they behaved civilly, and we parted as we had met, in a friendly manner. Before they left us they inquired of my men whether or not I was an Englishman, and being told that I was, they observed that the English were mad in their pursuit of beaver, since they could thus expose their lives for it; "for," added they, "the Upper Indians will certainly kill him," meaning myself. These Indians had left their village before the surrender

11

of Montreal and I was the first Englishman they had seen.

In conversation with my men I learned that the Algonquins of the Lake des Deux Montagnes, of which description were the party that I had now met, claim all the lands on the Outaouais as far as Lake Nipisingue; and that these lands are subdivided between their several Families upon whom they have devolved by inheritance. I was also informed that they are exceedingly strict as to the rights of property in this regard, accounting an invasion of them an offense sufficiently great to warrant the death of the invader.

We now reached the channels of the Grand Calumet, which lie amid numerous islands, and are about twenty miles in length. In this distance there are four carrying-places *(Portage Dufort, etc. -Author)* besides three or four *décharges (Décharge des Sables, etc. -Author)*, or *discharges*, which are places where the merchandise only is carried, and are therefore distinguishable from *portages*, or carrying-places where the canoe itself is taken out of the water and transported on men's shoulders. The four carrying-places included in the channels are short, with the exception of one, called the Portage de la Montagne, at which, besides its length, there is an acclivity of a hundred feet.

On the tenth of July* we reached the portage du Grand Calumet, which is at the head of the channels of the same name, and which name is derived from the *pièrre à Calumet*,** or pipe-stone, which here interrupts the river, occasioning a fall of water. This carrying-place is long and arduous, consisting in a high steep hill, over which the canoe cannot be carried by fewer than twelve men. The method of carrying the packages, or *pieces*, as they are called, is the same with that of the Indian Women, and which indeed is not peculiar even to them. One piece rests and hangs upon the shoulders, being suspended in a fillet, or forehead-band; and upon this is laid a second, which usually falls into the hollow of the neck, and assists the head in its support of the burden.

The ascent of this carrying-place is not more fatiguing than the descent is dangerous; and in performing it accidents too often occur, producing strains, ruptures, and injuries for life.***

The carrying-place and the repairs of our canoes, which cost us a day, detained us till the thirteenth. It is usual for the canoes to leave the Grand Calumet in good repair; the *rapids*, or shallow

---

*The month was now August. -Editor.

**The *pièrre à Calumet* is a compact limestone, yielding easily to the knife, and therefore employed for the bowls of tobacco pipes, both by the Indians and Canadians. -Author. Over two hundred of these pipes have been unearthed at Fort Michilimackinac. -Editor.

***A charitable fund is now established in Montreal for the relief of disabled and decayed *voyageurs.* -Author.

12

Falls of the Grand Calumet, on the Ottawa River. — Courtesy of Royal Ontario Museum, Toronto

Rapids de la Montagne, below the Grand Calumet. Courtesy of Royal Ontario Museum, Toronto

rocky parts of the channel (from which the canoes sustain the chief injury) being now passed, the current becomes gentle, and the carrying-places less frequent. The lands above the carrying-places and near the water are low, and in the spring entirely inundated.

On the morning of the fourteenth we reached a trading fort, or house, surrounded by a stockade, which had been built by the French, and at which the quantity of peltries received was once not inconsiderable. For twenty miles below this house the borders of the river are peculiarly well adapted to cultivation. From some Indians who were encamped near the house I purchased fish, dried and fresh.

At the rapids called Des Allumettes are two short carrying-places, above which is the *Rivière Creuse, (called by the English Deep River. -Author)* twenty-six miles in length, where the water flows with a gentle current at the foot of a high, mountainous, barren and rocky country on the north, and has a low and sandy soil on the south. On this southern side is a remarkable point of sand, stretching far into the stream, and on which it is customary to baptize novices. Above the River Creuse are the two carrying-places of the length of half a mile each, called the Portages des Deux Joachins; and at fifteen miles farther, at the mouth of the

1760 Map

of the

Straits of Mackinac

14

River Du Moine is another fort, or trading-house, where I found a small encampment of Indians called Maskegons, and with whom I bartered several articles for furs. They anxiously inquired whether or not the English were in possession of the country below, and whether or not, if they were, they would allow traders to come to that trading-house; declaring that their families must starve unless they should be able to procure ammunition and other necessaries. I answered both these questions in the affirmative, at which they expressed much satisfaction.

Above the Moine are several strong and dangerous rapids, reaching to the Portage du Roche Capitaine, a carrying-place of three-quarters of a mile in length, mountainous, rocky, and wooded only with stunted pine trees and spruce. Above this is the Portage des Deux Rivières, so called from the two small rivers by which it is intersected; and higher still are many rapids and shoals, called by the Indians *matawa*.* Here the river, called by the French Petite Rivière, and by the Indians Matawa Sipi, falls into the Outaouais. We now left the latter of these rivers and proceeded to ascend the Matawa* [Matawan River].

---

*Mataouan (Matawan); *Charlevoix*; Matawoen. — Mackenzie's *Voyages.* -Author.

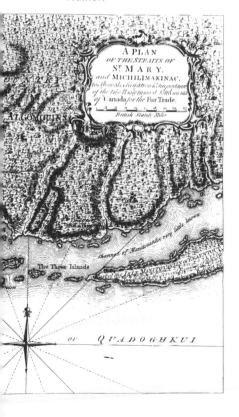

3

ONWARD *to* MICHILIMACKINAC

Our course in ascending the Outaouais had been west-north-west; but on entering the Matawa our faces were turned to the southwest. This latter river is computed to be fourteen leagues in length. In the widest parts it is a hundred yards broad, and in others not more than fifty. In ascending it there are fourteen carrying-places and discharges, of which some are extremely difficult. Its banks are almost two continuous rocks, with scarcely earth enough for the burial of a dead body. I saw Indian graves, if graves they might be called, where the corpse was laid upon the bare rock and covered with stones. In the side of a hill on the north side of the river there is a curious cave concerning which marvelous tales are related by the *voyageurs*. Mosquitoes and a minute species of black fly abound on this river, the latter of which are still more troublesome than the former. To obtain a respite from their vexations we were obliged at the carrying-places to make fires and stand in the smoke.

On the twenty-sixth of August we reached the Portages à la Vase, [the Muddy Portages] three in number, and each two miles in length. Their name describes the boggy ground of which they consist. In passing one of them we saw many beaver houses and dams; and by breaking one of the dams we let off water enough to float our canoes down a small stream which would not otherwise have been navigable. These carrying-places and the intermediate navigation brought us at length to the head of a small river which falls into Lake Nipisingue. We had now passed the country of which the streams fall northeastward into the Outaouais, and entered that from which they flow in a contrary direction toward Lake Huron. On one side of the *height of land,* which is the reciprocal boundary of these regions, we had left Lake aux Tourtres and the River Matawa; and before us on the other was Lake Nipisingue. The banks of the little river by which we descended into the lake, and more especially as we approached the lake, were of an exceedingly delightful appearance, covered with high grass and affording an extensive prospect. Both the lake and river abound in black bass, sturgeon, pike, and other fish. Among the pike is to be included the species called by the Indians *masquinonge* [Muskellunge]. In two hours with the assistance of an Indian we took as much fish as all the party could eat.

Lake Nipisingue is distant two hundred leagues from Montreal. Its circumference is said to measure one hundred and fifty miles, and its depth is sufficient for vessels of any burden. On our voyage along its eastern banks we met some canoes of Indians, who said they lived on the northwestern side. My men informed me that they were Nipisingues, a name which they derive from the lake. Their language is a dialect of the Algonquin; and by nation they are a mixture of Chippewa and Maskegons. They had a large quantity of furs, part of which I purchased. The animals which the country affords them are the beaver, marten, bear and *o'tic, a'tic,* or *caribou,* a species of deer, by some called the *reindeer.* They wished for rum, but I avoided selling or giving them any.

Leaving the Indians, we proceeded to the mouth of the lake at which is the carrying-place of La Chaudière Française *(or, la Chaudière des Français. -Author.),* a name part of which it has obtained from the holes in the rock over which we passed; and which holes, being of the kind which is known to be formed by water with the assistance of pebbles, demonstrate that it has not always been dry as at present it is, but the phenomenon is not peculiar to this spot, the same being observable at almost every carrying-place on the Outaouais. At the height of a hundred feet above the river I commonly found pebbles worn into a round form like those upon the beach below. Everywhere the water appears to have subsided from its ancient levels; and imagination may anticipate an era at which even the banks of Newfoundland will be left bare.

The southern shores of Lake Nipisingue are rocky, and only thinly covered with pine trees and spruce, both, as in several instances already mentioned, of a small stature. The carrying-place of La Chaudière Française is at the head of the River des Français, and where the water first descends from the level of Lake Nipisingue toward that of Lake Huron. This it does not reach till it has passed down many rapids, full of danger to the canoes and the men, after which it enters Lake Huron by several arms, flowing through each as through mill-race. The River des Français [French River] is twenty leagues in length and has many islands in its channel. Its banks are uniformly of rock. Among the carrying-places at which we successively arrived are

River des Francais. — Courtesy of Royal Ontario Museum, Toronto

Portage de la Petite Faucille on the River des Francais. — Courtesy of Royal Ontario Museum

the Portage des Pins, or du Pin; de la Grande Faucille; de la Petite Faucille *(Faucille, Fr. a sickle -Author)*; and du Sault du Recolet.* Near the mouth of the river a meadow, called La Prairie des Français, varies for a short space the rocky surface which so generally prevails; and on this spot we encamped and repaired our canoes. The carrying-places are now all passed, and what remained was to cross the billows of Lake Huron, which lay stretched across our horizon like an ocean.

On the thirty-first day of August we entered the lake, the waves running high from the south, and breaking over numerous rocks. At first I thought the prospect alarming; but the canoes rode on the water with the ease of a sea-bird, and my apprehensions ceased. We passed Point de Grondines, so called from the perpetual noise of the water among the rocks. Many of these rocks are sunken and not without danger when the wind, as at this time it was, is from the south.

We coasted along many small islands, or rather rocks, of more or less extent, either wholly bare or very scantily covered with scrub pine trees. All the land to the northward is of the same description as high as Cha'ba' bou'an'ing, where verdure reappears.

On the following day we reached an island called LaCloche, because there is here a rock standing on a plain, which, being struck, rings like a bell.

I found the island inhabited by a large village of Indians, whose behavior was at first full of civility and kindness. I bartered away some small articles among them in exchange for fish and dried meat; and we remained upon friendly terms till, discovering that I was an Englishman, they told my men that the Indians at Michilimackinac would not fail to kill me, and that therefore they had a right to a share of the pillage. Upon this principle, as they said, they demanded a keg of rum, adding that if not given them they would proceed to take it. I judged it prudent to comply; on condition, however, that I should experience at this place no further molestation.

The condition was not unfaithfully observed; but the repeated warnings which I had now received of sure destruction at Michilimackinac could not but oppress my mind. I could not even yield myself, without danger, to the course suggested by my fears; for my provisions were nearly exhausted and to return was, therefore, almost impracticable.

---

*So called, perhaps, on account of the resemblance of this Sault to that of the *Sault* du Recolet, between the islands of Montreal and Jesus, and which has its name from the death of a Recolet or Franciscan friar, who was there drowned. -Author.

The hostility of the Indians was exclusively against the English. Between them and my Canadian attendants there appeared the most cordial good-will. This circumstance suggested one means of escape, of which by the advice of my friend Campion I resolved to attempt availing myself; and which was that of putting on the dress usually worn by such of the Canadians as pursue the trade into which I had entered and assimilating myself as much as I was able to their appearance and manners. To this end I laid aside my English clothes and covered myself only with a cloth passed about the middle, a shirt hanging loose, a molton, or blanket coat, and a large, red, milled worsted cap. The next thing was to smear my face and hands with dirt and grease; and this done, I took the place of one of my men, and when Indians approached, used the paddle with as much skill as I possessed. I had the satisfaction to find that my disguise enabled me to pass several canoes without attracting the smallest notice.

In this manner I pursued my voyage to the mouth, or rather mouths, of the Missisaki, a river which descends from the north, and of which the name imports that it has several mouths or outlets. From this river all the Indians inhabiting the north side of Lake Huron are called Missisakies. There is here a plentiful sturgeon fishery, by which those that resort to it are fed during the summer months. On our voyage we met several Missisakies of whom we bought fish and from whose stock we might easily have filled all our canoes.

From the Missisaki, which is on the north shore of Lake Huron, to Michilimackinac, which is on the south, is reckoned thirty leagues. The lake, which here approaches Lake Superior, is now contracted in its breadth, as well as filled with islands. From the mouth of the River des Français to the Missisaki is reckoned fifty leagues, with many islands along the route. The lands everywhere from the Island of La Cloche are poor, with the exception of those of the Island of Manitoualin, a hundred miles in length,* where they are generally good. On all the islands the Indians cultivate small quantities of maize.

---

*The Isle Manitoualin was formerly so described. It is now known that there is no island in Lake Huron of a hundred miles in length, and that the *Manitoualin* are a chain of islands. The French writers on Canada speak of the Isle Manitoualin as inhabited in their time by the Amikoues (Amicways, Amicwac), whom they called a family (and sometimes a nation), deriving its origin from the Great Beaver, a personage of mythological importance. The name *Manitoualin* implies the residence of *Manitoes*, or genii, a distinction very commonly attributed to the islands, and sometimes to the shores, of Lakes Huron and Superior, and of which further examples will present themselves in the course of these pages. -Author.

20

From the Missisaki we proceeded to the O'tossalon* and thence across the lake, making one island after another, at intervals of from two to three leagues. The lake, as far as it could be seen, tended to the westward and became less and less broad.

The first land which we made on the south shore was that called Point du Détour or Grand Détour, after which we passed the island called Isle aux Outardes [Goose Island], and then leaving on the right the deep bay of Boutchitaouy came to the island of Michilimackinac, distant from Isle aux Outardes three leagues. On our way a sudden squall reduced us to the point of throwing over the cargoes of our canoes to save the latter from filling; but the wind subsided and we reached the island in safety.

The land in the center of this island is high and its form somewhat resembles that of a turtle's back. Mackinac, or Mickinac, signifies a *turtle*, and *michi (mishi)*, or *missi*, signifies *great*, as it does also *several*, or *many*. The common interpretation of the word *Michilimackinac* is the Great Turtle. It is from this island that the fort, commonly known by the name of Michilimackinac, has obtained its appellation.

On the island, as I had been previously taught to expect, there was a village of Chippewa, said to contain a hundred warriors. Here I was fearful of discovery and consequent ill-treatment, but after inquiring the news, and particularly whether or not any Englishman was coming to Michilimackinac, they suffered us to pass uninjured. One man, indeed, looked at me, laughed, and pointed me out to another. This was enough to give me some uneasiness; but whatever was the singularity he perceived in me, both he and his friend retired without suspecting me to be an Englishman.

Mackinac Island is shaped like a great turtle. This 1842 drawing shows: Fort Mackinac which was not built until 1780. — Courtesy of Chicago Historical Society

*Also written *Tessalon, Thessalon,* and *des Tessalons.* -Author.

21

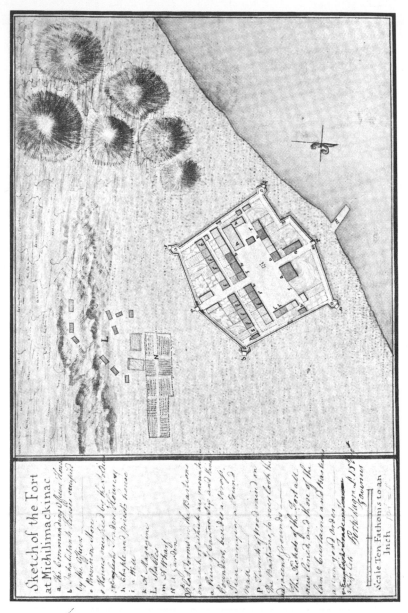

Lt. Perkins Magra's map of Fort Michilimackinac as drawn in 1766, three years after the massacre. —Courtesy of William L. Clements Library, University of Michigan

4

ARRIVAL at
MICHILIMACKINAC

Leaving as speedily as possible the island of Michilimackinac I crossed the strait and landed at the fort of the same name. The distance from the island is about two leagues. I landed at four o'clock in the afternoon.

Here I put the entire charge of my effects into the hands of my assistant, Campion, between whom and myself it had been previously agreed that he should pass for the proprietor; and my men were instructed to conceal the fact that I was an Englishman.

Campion soon found a house to which I retired, and where I hoped to remain in privacy; but the men soon betrayed my secret, and I was visited by the inhabitants with great show of civility. They assured me that I could not stay at Michilimackinac without the most imminent risk; and strongly recommended that I should lose no time in making my escape to Detroit.

Though language like this could not but increase my uneasiness it did not shake my determination to remain with my property and encounter the evils with which I was threatened; and my spirits were in some measure sustained by the sentiments of Campion in this regard; for he declared his belief that the Canadian inhabitants of the fort were more hostile than the Indians as being jealous of English traders; who like myself were penetrating into the country.

Fort Michilimackinac was built [in 1715] by order of the governor-general of Canada and garrisoned with a small number of militia who, having families, soon became less soldiers than settlers. Most of those whom I found in the fort had originally served in the French army.

The fort stands on the south side of the strait which is between Lake Huron and Lake Michigan. It has an area of two acres, and is enclosed with pickets of cedar wood *(Thuya occidentalis. -Author)*; and it is so near the water's edge that when

23

the wind is in the west the waves break against the stockade. On the bastions are two small pieces of brass English cannon taken some years since [1686] by a party of Canadians [led by Chevalier de Troyes] who went on a plundering expedition against the posts of Hudson's Bay, which they reached by the route of the River Churchill.

Within the stockade are thirty houses, neat in their appearance, and tolerably commodious; and a church in which mass is celebrated by a Jesuit missionary.* The number of families may be nearly equal to that of the houses; and their subsistence is derived from the Indian traders who assemble here in their voyages to and from Montreal. Michilimackinac is the place of deposit and point of departure between the upper countries and the lower. Here the outfits are prepared for the countries of Lake Michigan and the Mississippi, Lake Superior, and the Northwest; and here the returns in furs are collected and embarked for Montreal.

I was not released from the visits and admonitions of the inhabitants of the fort before I received the equivocal intelligence that the whole band of Chippewa from the island of Michilimackinac was arrived with the intention of paying me a visit.

There was in the fort one [Jacques Philippe] Farley, an interpreter, lately in the employ of the French commandant. He had married a Chippewa woman and was said to possess great influence over the nation to which his wife belonged. Doubtful as to the kind of visit which I was about to receive, I sent for this interpreter and requested first that he would inform me of the intentions of the band. M. Farley agreed to be present; and as to the object of the visit, replied that it was consistent with uniform custom that a stranger on his arrival should be waited upon and welcomed by the chiefs of the nation, who on their part always gave a small present, and always expected a large one; but as to the rest, declared himself unable to answer for the particular views of the Chippewa on this occasion, I being an Englishman, and the Indians having made no treaty with the English. He thought that there might be danger, the Indians having protested that they would not suffer an Englishman to remain in their part of the country. This information was far from agreeable; but there was no resource, except in fortitude and patience.

At two o'clock in the afternoon the Chippewa came to my house, about sixty in number, and headed by Minavavana, their chief. They walked in single file, each with his tomahawk in one

---

*The church of Ste. Anne de Michilimackinac was reconstructed on its original site in 1964. -Editor.

24

hand and scalping knife in the other. Their bodies were naked from the waist upward, except in a few examples where blankets were thrown loosely over the shoulders. Their faces were painted with charcoal, worked up with grease; their bodies with white clay in patterns of various fancies. Some had feathers thrust through their noses, and their heads decorated with the same. It is unnecessary to dwell on the sensations with which I beheld the approach of this uncouth, if not frightful assemblage.

The chief entered first, and the rest followed without noise. On receiving a sign from the former, the latter seated themselves on the floor.

Minavavana [the Grand Sauteur] appeared to be about fifty years of age. He was six feet in height and had in his countenance an indescribable mixture of good and evil. Looking steadfastly at me where I sat in ceremony, with an interpreter on either hand, and several Canadians behind me, he entered at the same time into conversation with Campion, inquiring how long it was since I left Montreal, and observing that the English, as it would seem, were brave men and not afraid of death, since they dared to come as I had done fearlessly among their enemies.

The Indians now gravely smoked their pipes, while I inwardly endured the tortures of suspense. At length the pipes being finished, as well as the long pause by which they were succeeded, Minavavana, taking a few strings of wampum in his hand, began the following speech:

"Englishman, it is to you that I speak, and I demand your attention.

"Englishman, you know that the French king is our father. He promised to be such; and we in return promised to be his children. This promise we have kept.

"Englishman, it is you that have made war with this our father. You are his enemy; and how then could you have the boldness to venture among us, his children? You know that his enemies are ours.

"Englishman, we are informed that our father, the King of France, is old and infirm; and that being fatigued with making war upon your nation, he is fallen asleep. During his sleep you have taken advantage of him and possessed yourselves of Canada. But his nap is almost at an end. I think I hear him already stirring and inquiring for his children, the Indians; and when he does awake, what must become of you? He will destroy you utterly.

"Englishman, although you have conquered the French, you have not yet conquered us. We are not your slaves. These lakes, these woods and mountains were left to us by our ancestors. They are our inheritance; and we will part with them to none. Your nation supposes that we, like the white people, cannot live

CHIPPEWA WARRIOR

without bread—and pork—and beef. But you ought to know that He, the Great Spirit and Master of Life, has provided food for us in these spacious lakes and on these woody mountains.

"Englishman, our father, the King of France, employed our young men to make war upon your nation. In this warfare many of them have been killed, and it is our custom to retaliate until such time as the spirits of the slain are satisfied. But spirits of the slain are to be satisfied in either of two ways; the first is by the spilling of the blood of the nation by which they fell; the other by *covering the bodies of the dead*, and thus allaying the resentment of their relations. This is done by making presents.

"Englishman, your king has never sent us any presents, nor entered into any treaty with us, wherefore he and we are still at war; and until he does these things we must consider that we have no other father, nor friend among the white men than the King of France; but for you we have taken into consideration that you have ventured your life among us in the expectation that we should not molest you. You do not come armed with an intention to make war; you come in peace to trade with us and supply us with necessaries of which we are in much want. We shall regard you, therefore, as a brother; and you may sleep tranquilly, without fear of the Chippewa. As a token of our friendship we present you with this pipe to smoke."

As Minavavana uttered these words an Indian presented me with a pipe, which, after I had drawn the smoke three times, was carried to the chief, and after him to every person in the room. This ceremony ended, the chief arose and gave me his hand in which he was followed by all the rest.

Being again seated, Minavavana requested that his young men might be allowed to taste what he called my *English milk* (meaning *rum*)—observing that it was long since they had tasted any, and that they were very desirous to know whether or not there were any difference between the English milk and the French.

My adventure on leaving Fort William Augustus had left an impression on my mind which made me tremble when Indians asked for rum; and I would therefore willingly have excused myself in this particular; but being informed that it was customary to comply with the request, and withal satisfied with the friendly declarations which I had received, I promised to give them a small cask at parting.

After this, by the aid of my interpreter I made a reply to the speech of Minavavana, declaring that it was the good character which I had heard of the Indians that had alone emboldened me to come among them; that their late father the King of France, had surrendered Canada to the King of England, whom they ought now to regard as their father, and who would be as

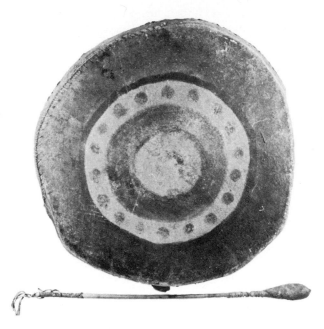

Indian drum and drumstick

Indian Catlinite pipe from Michilimackinac. — Courtesy of City of Liverpool Museums

careful of them as the other had been; that I had come to furnish them with necessaries, and that their good treatment of me would be an encouragement to others. They appeared satisfied with what I said, repeating *eh!* (an expression of approbation) after hearing each particular. I had prepared a present which I now gave them with the utmost good will. At their departure I distributed a small quantity of rum.

Relieved as I now imagined myself from all occasion of anxiety as to the treatment which I was to experience from the Indians, I assorted my goods, and hired Canadian interpreters and clerks, in whose care I was to send them into Lake Michigan and the River St. Pierre [Minnesota River], in the country of the Nadowessies [Sioux]; into Lake Superior among the Chippewa, and to the Grand Portage for the Northwest. Everything was ready for their departure when new dangers sprung up and threatened to overwhelm me.

At the entrance of Lake Michigan and at about twenty miles to the West of Fort Michilimackinac is the village of L'Arbre Croche [the Crooked Tree, near modern Cross Village], inhabited by a band of Ottawa boasting of two hundred and fifty fighting men. L'Arbre Croche is the seat of the Jesuit mission of St. Ignace de Michilimackinac, and the people are partly baptized, and partly not. The missionary resides on a farm attached to the mission and situated between the village and the fort, both of which are under his care. The Ottawa of L'Arbre Croche, who when compared with the Chippewa appear to be much advanced in civilization, grow maize for the market of Michilimackinac, where this commodity is depended upon for provisioning the canoes.

The new dangers which presented themselves came from this village of Ottawa. Everything as I have said was in readiness for the departure of my goods when accounts arrived of its approach; and shortly after, two hundred warriors entered the fort and billeted themselves in the several houses among the Canadian inhabitants. The next morning they assembled in the house which was built for the commandant, or governor, and ordered the attendance of myself and of two other merchants still later from Montreal, namely Messrs. [James] Stanley Goddard and Ezekiel Solomons.

After our entering the council room and taking our seats one of the chiefs commenced an address:

"Englishmen," said he, "we, the Ottawas were some time since informed of your arrival in this country, and of your having brought with you the goods of which we have need. At this news we were greatly pleased, believing that through your assistance our wives and children would be enabled to pass another winter; but what was our surprise, when a few days ago we were again informed that the goods which as we had expected were intended for us were on the eve of departure for distant countries, of which some are inhabited by our enemies. These accounts being spread, our wives and children came to us crying and desiring that we should go to the fort to learn with our own ears their truth or falsehood. We accordingly embarked almost naked as you see; and on our arrival here we have inquired into the accounts and found them true. We see your canoes ready to depart and find your men engaged for the Mississippi and other distant regions.

"Under these circumstances we have considered the affair; and you are now sent for that you may hear our determination, which is that you shall give to each of our men, young and old, merchandise and ammunition to the amount of fifty beaver skins on credit, and for which I have no doubt of their paying you in the summer, on their return from their wintering."

A compliance with this demand would have stripped me and my fellow merchants of all our merchandise; and what rendered the affair still more serious, we even learned that these Ottawa were accustomed never to pay for what they received on credit. In reply, therefore, to the speech which we had heard, we requested that the demand contained in it might be diminished; but we were answered that the Ottawa had nothing further to say except that they would allow till the next day for reflection; after which, if compliance was not given, they would make no further application, but take into their own hands the property which they already regarded as their own—as having been brought into their country before the conclusion of any peace between themselves and the English.

We now returned to consider of our situation; and in the evening Farley, the interpreter, paid us a visit, and assured us that it was the intention of the Ottawa to put us that night to death. He advised us, as our only means of safety, to comply with the demands which had been made; but we suspected our informant of a disposition to prey upon our fears with a view to induce us to abandon the Indian trade, and resolved however this might be, rather to stand on the defensive than submit. We trusted to the house in which I lived as a fort, and armed ourselves and about thirty of our men with muskets. Whether or not the Ottawa ever intended violence we never had an opportunity of knowing; but the night passed quietly.

Early the next morning a second council was held, and the merchants were again summoned to attend. Believing that every hope of resistance would be lost, should we commit our persons into the hands of our enemies, we sent only a refusal. There was none without in whom we had any confidence, except Campion.

From him we learned from time to time whatever was rumored among the Canadian inhabitants as to the designs of the Ottawa; and from him toward sunset we received the gratifying intelligence that a detachment of British soldiery, sent to garrison Michilimackinac, was distant only five miles and would enter the fort early the next morning.

Near at hand, however, as relief was reported to be, our anxiety could not but be great; for a long night was to be passed, and our fate might be decided before the morning. To increase our apprehensions, about midnight we were informed that the Ottawa were holding a council, at which no white man was permitted to be present, Farley alone excepted; and him we suspected, and afterward positively knew to be our greatest enemy. We, on our part, remained all night upon the alert; but at daybreak to our surprise and joy we saw the Ottawa preparing to depart. By sunrise not a man of them was left in the fort; and indeed the scene was altogether changed. The inhabitants, who, while the Ottawa were present, had avoided all connection with the English traders, now came with congratulations. They related that the Ottawa had proposed to them that if joined by the Canadians they would march and attack the troops which were known to be advancing on the fort; and they added that it was their refusal which had determined the Ottawa to depart.

At noon [September 28, 1761] three hundred troops of the Sixtieth Regiment, under the command of Lieutenant Lesslie, marched into the fort; and this arrival dissipated all our fears from whatever source derived.*

After a few days detachments were sent into the Bay des Puants [Green Day] by which is the route to the Mississippi and at the mouth of the St. Joseph which leads to the Illinois. The Indians from all quarters came to pay their respects to the commandant; and the merchants dispatched their canoes, though it was now the middle of September, and therefore somewhat late in the season.

---

*Captain Henry Balfour of the Eightieth Regiment was actually in command. Within a short time, however, he departed with most of the troops leaving Lieutenant Leslie of the Sixtieth Regiment-The Royal Americans — in charge of the twenty-eight man garrison at Michilimackinac. -Editor.

Soldiers passed the long winter days with gambling and games

The priest was a welcome visitor in the homes of Michilimackinac.

5
WINTER
at
MICHILIMACKINAC

The village of L'Arbre Croche supplies, as I have said, the maize, or *Indian corn*, with which the canoes are victualled. This species of grain is prepared for use by boiling it in a strong lye, after which the husk may be easily removed; and it is next mashed and dried. In this state it is soft and friable like rice. The allowance for each man on the voyage is a quart a day; and a bushel with two pounds of prepared fat is reckoned to be a month's subsistence. No other allowance is made of any kind, not even of salt; and bread is never thought of. The men, nevertheless, are healthy and capable of performing their heavy labor. This mode of victualling is essential to the trade, which being pursued at great distances, and in vessels so small as canoes, will not admit of the use of other food. If the men were to be supplied with bread and pork the canoes could not carry a sufficiency for six months; and the ordinary duration of the voyage is not less than fourteen. The difficulty which would belong to an attempt to reconcile any other men than Canadians to this fare seems to secure to them and their employers the monopoly of the fur trade.

The sociable disposition of the commandant enabled us to pass the winter at Michilimackinac in a manner as agreeable as circumstances would permit. The amusements consisted chiefly in shooting, hunting, and fishing. The neighboring woods abounded in *partridges** and hares, the latter of which is white in winter; and the lake is filled with fish, of which the most celebrated are trout, whitefish, and sturgeon.

Trout are taken by making holes in the ice in which are set lines and baits. These are often left for many days together, and in some places at the depth of fifty fathoms; for the trout having

---

*In North-America there is no *partridge*; but the name is given to more than one species of grouse. The birds here intended, are red grouse. -Author.

swallowed the bait, remains fast and alive till taken up. This fish, which is found of the weight of from ten to sixty pounds and upward, constitutes the principal food of the inhabitants.* When this fails they have recourse to maize, but this is very expensive. I bought more than a hundred bushels at forty livres per bushel. Money is rarely received or paid at Michilimackinac, the circulating medium consisting in furs and peltries.** In this exchange a pound of beaver skin is reckoned at sixty sols [two shillings six pence], an otter skin at six livres [six shillings], and marten skins at thirty sols each [one shilling six pence]. This is only one-half of the real value of the furs; and it is therefore always agreed to pay either in furs at their actual price at the fort, or in cash to double the amount, as reckoned in furs.

At the same time that I paid the price which I have mentioned for maize I paid at the rate of a dollar per pound for the tallow, or prepared fat to mix with it. The meat itself was at the same price. The Jesuit missionary killed an ox which he sold by the quarter, taking the weight of the meat in beaver skin. Beaver skin as just intimated, was worth a dollar per pound.

These high prices of grain and beef led me to be very industrious in fishing. I usually set twenty lines and visited them daily, and often found at every visit fish enough to feed a hundred men. Whitefish, which exceed the trout as a delicious and nutritive food, are here in astonishing numbers. In shape they somewhat resemble the shad, but their flavor is perhaps above all comparison whatever. Those who live on them for months together preserve their relish to the end. This cannot be said of the trout.

The whitefish is taken in nets which are set under the ice. To do this several holes are made in the ice, each at such distance from that behind it as that it may be reached under the ice by the end of a pole. A line of sixty fathoms in length is thus conveyed from hole to hole till it is extended to the length desired. This done, the pole is taken out, and with it one end of the line, to which the end is then fastened. The line being now drawn back by an assistant who holds the opposite extremity, the net is brought under and a large stone is made fast to the sinking line at each end and let down to the bottom; and the net is spread in the water by lighters on its upper edge, sinkers on its lower, in the usual manner. The fish, running against the net, entangle their gills in the meshes and are thus detained till taken up. Whitefish is used as a bait for trout. They are much smaller

---

*The prodigious quantity of fish bones unearthed at Michilimackinac attests Henry's observation. -Editor.

**Only a few French, Spanish and English coins have been found at Michilimackinac and most of these are nearly worn smooth. -Editor.

34

than the trout, but usually weigh, at Michilimackinac, from three to seven pounds.

During the whole winter very few Indians visited the fort; but two families, one of which was that of a chief, had their lodges on a river five leagues below us, and occasionally brought beaver flesh for sale.*

The chief was warmly attached to the English. He had been taken prisoner by Sir William Johnson at the siege of Fort Niagara, and had received from that intelligent officer his liberty, the medal usually presented to a chief, and the British flag. Won by these unexpected acts of kindness, he had returned to Michilimackinac full of praises of the English, and hoisting his flag over his lodge. This latter demonstration of his partiality had nearly cost him his life; his lodge was broken down and his flag torn to pieces. The pieces he carefully gathered up and preserved with pious care; and whenever he came to the fort he drew them forth and exhibited them. On these occasions it grew into a custom to give him as much liquor as he said was necessary to make him cry over the misfortune of losing his flag. The commandant would have given him another, but he thought that he could not accept it without danger.

The greatest depth of snow throughout the season was three feet. On the second day of April the ice on the lake broke up and the navigation was resumed; and we immediately began to receive from the Indians around us large supplies of wild fowl.

Fort Michilimackinac in winter

*A surprising quantity of beaver bones have been found in the garbage pits inside Fort Michilimackinac. -Editor.

Fort Michilimackinac Land-gate entrance

6

A VOYAGE

to

SAULT SAINTE MARIE

Being desirous of visiting the Sault de Ste. Marie I left Michilimackinac on the fifteenth of May in a canoe. The Sault de Ste. Marie is distant from Michilimackinac thirty leagues and lies in the strait which separated Lake Huron from Lake Superior.

Having passed Le Détour, a point of land at the entrance of the strait, our course lay among numerous islands, some of which are twenty miles in length. We ascended the *rapid* of Miscoutin-saki, a spot well adapted for mill seats, and above which is the mouth of the river of the same name. The lands on the south shore of this river are excellent. The lake is bordered by meadows, and at a short distance back are groves of sugar maple. From this river to the Sault de Ste. Marie is one continued meadow.

On the nineteenth I reached the Sault. Here was a stockaded fort in which under the French government there was kept a small garrison, commanded by an officer who was called *the governor*, but was in fact a clerk who managed the Indian trade here on government account. The houses were four in number, of which the first was the governor's, the second the interpreter's, and the other two, which were the smallest, had been used for barracks. The only family was that of M. [Jean Baptiste] Cadotte, the interpreter, whose wife was a Chippewa.

The fort is seated on a beautiful plain of about two miles in circumference, and covered with luxuriant grass; and within sight are the *rapids* in the strait, distant half a mile. The width of the strait, or river, is about half a mile. The *portage*, or carrying-place, commences at the fort. The banks are rocky, and allow only a narrow footpath over them. Canoes, half loaded, ascend on the south side and the other half of the load is carried on men's shoulders.

These *rapids* are beset with rocks of the most dangerous description; and yet they are the scene of a fishery in which all their dangers are braved and mastered with singular expertness. They are full of whitefish much larger and more excellent than those of Michilimackinac, and which are found here during the greater part of the season, weighing in general from six pounds to fifteen.

The method of taking them is this: each canoe carries two men, one of whom steers with a paddle, and the other is provided with a pole ten feet in length, and at the end of which is affixed a scoop-net. The steersman sets the canoe from the eddy of one rock to that of another; while the fisherman in the prow, who sees through the pellucid element the prey of which he is in pursuit, dips his net and sometimes brings up at every succeeding dip as many as it can contain. The fish are often crowded together in the water in great numbers, and a skillful fisherman in autumn will take five hundred in two hours.

This fishery is of great moment to the surrounding Indians, whom it supplies with a large proportion of their winter's provision; for having taken the fish in the manner described, they cure them by drying in the smoke, and lay them up in large quantities.

There is at present a village of Chippewa of fifty warriors seated at this place; but the inhabitants reside here during the summer only, going westward in the winter to hunt. The village was anciently much more populous.

At the south are also seen a few of the wandering *O'pimittish Ininiwac*, literally Men of the Woods, otherwise called Wood Indians and *Gens de Terres* — a peaceable and inoffensive race, but less conversant with some of the arts of first necessity than any of their neighbors. They have no villages, and their lodges are so rudely fashioned as to afford them but very inadequate protection against inclement skies. The greater part of their year is spent in traveling from place to place in search of food. The animal on which they chiefly depend is the hare. This they take in springes. Of the skin they make coverings with much ingenuity, cutting it into narrow strips, and weaving these into a cloth of the shape of a blanket, and of a quality very warm and agreeable.

The pleasant situation of the fort, and still more the desire of learning the Chippewa language, led me to resolve on wintering in it. In the family of M. Cadotte no other language than the Chippewa was spoken.

During the summer the weather was sometimes exceedingly hot. Mosquitoes and black flies were so numerous as to be a heavy counterpoise to the pleasure of hunting. Pigeons were in great plenty; the stream supplied our drink; and sickness was unknown.

In the course of the season a small detachment of troops under the command of Lieutenant [John] Jemette [of the Sixtieth Regiment] arrived to garrison the fort.

7

DISASTER *and* RETURN

In the beginning of October the fish as is usual was in great abundance at the Sault; and by the fifteenth day of the month I had myself taken upward of five hundred. These I caused to be dried in the customary manner by suspending them in pairs, head downward, on long poles laid horizontally for that purpose and supported by two stakes driven into the ground at either end. The fish are frozen the first night after they are taken; and by the aid of the severe cold of the winter they are thus preserved in a state perfectly fit for use even till the month of April.

Others were not less successful than myself; and several canoe-loads of fish were exported to Michilimackinac, our commanding officer being unable to believe that his troops would have need to live on fish during the winter; when, as he flattered himself, a regular supply of venison and other food would reach the garrison through the means of the Indians, whose services he proposed to purchase out of the large funds of liquor which were subject to his orders.

But all these calculations were defeated by the arrival of a very serious misfortune. At one o'clock in the morning of the twenty-second day of December I was awakened by an alarm of fire, which was actually raging in the houses of the commandant and others. On arriving at the commandant's I found that this officer was still within side; and being acquainted with the window of the room in which he slept I procured it to be broken in, in time for his escape. I was also so fortunate as to save a small quantity of gunpowder only a few moments before the fire reached all the remainder. A part of the stockade, all the houses, M. Cadotte's alone excepted, all the provisions of the troops, and a considerable part of our fish were burnt.

On consultation the next day it was agreed that the only means which remained at this late period of the season to preserve the garrison from famine was that of sending it back to Michilimackinac. This was itself an undertaking of some peril; for, had the ice prevented their reaching the place of destination, starving would have become as inevitable elsewhere as it threatened to be at the Sault de Ste. Marie. The soldiers embarked and happily reached Michilimackinac on the thirty-first day of the month. On the very next morning the navigation was wholly closed.

The commandant and all the rest now lived in one small house, subsisting only by hunting and fishing. The woods afforded us some hares and partridges, and we took large trout with the spear. In order to spear trout under the ice, holes being first cut of two yards in circumference, cabins of about two feet in height are built over them of small branches of trees; and these are further covered with skins so as wholly to exclude the light. The design and result of this contrivance is to render it practicable to discern objects in the water at a very considerable depth; for the reflection of light from the water gives that element an opaque appearance and hides all objects from the eye at a small distance beneath its surface. A spear head of iron is fastened on a pole of about ten feet in length. This instrument is lowered into the water; and the fisherman, lying upon his belly, with his head under the cabin or cover, and therefore over the hole, lets down the figure of a fish in wood and filled with lead. Round the middle of the fish is tied a small packthread; and when at the depth of ten fathoms where it is intended to be employed, it is made, by drawing the string and by the simultaneous pressure of the water, to move forward after the manner of a real fish. Trout and other large fish, deceived by its resemblance, spring toward it to seize it; but by a dexterous jerk of the string it is instantly taken out of their reach. The decoy is now drawn nearer to the surface, and the fish takes some time to renew the attack, during which the spear is raised and held conveniently for striking. On the return of the fish the spear is plunged into its back; and the spear being barbed, it is easily drawn out of the water. So completely do the rays of the light pervade the element that in three fathoms of water I have often seen the shadows of the fish on the bottom, following them as they moved; and this when the ice itself was two feet in thickness.

By these pursuits and others of a similar kind we supported ourselves for two months, that is until the twentieth of February, when we imagined the lake to be frozen and Michilimackinac therefore accessible; and the commandant wishing to go to that fort, M. Cadotte, myself, two Canadians, and two Indians, agreed to accompany him. The Canadians and Indians were loaded with some parched maize, some fish, a few pieces of scorched pork, which had been saved from the fire, and a few loaves of bread made of flour which was also partly burnt.

We walked on snowshoes, a mode of traveling sufficiently fatiguing to myself, but of which the commandant had had no previous experience whatever. In consequence our progress was slow, wearisome, and disastrous. On the seventh day of our march we had only reached Point du Détour which lies half way between the Sault and Michilimackinac; and here to our mortification and dismay we found the lake still open and the ice drifting. Our provisions, too, on examination, were found to be nearly expended; and nothing remained for us to do but to send back the Canadians and Indians, whose motions would be swift, for an additional supply.

In their absence the commandant, M. Cadotte, and myself, three persons in number, were left with about two pounds of pork and three of bread for our subsistence during the three days and perhaps four, which they would require for a journey of ninety miles. Being appointed to act the part of commissary, I divided the provisions into four parts, one for each day; and to our great happiness at ten o'clock on the fourth day our faithful servants returned. Early in the morning of the fifth we left our encampment and proceeded. The weather this day was exceedingly cold.

We had only advanced two leagues when the commandant found it almost wholly impossible to go further, his feet being blistered by the cords of the snowshoes. On this account we made short marches for three days; and this loss of time threatened us anew with famine. We were now too far from the Sault to send back for a supply; and it was therefore determined that myself, accompanied by one of the Canadians, should go as speedily as possible to Michilimackinac, and there inform the commanding officer of the situation of those behind. Accordingly the next morning at break of day I left my fellow sufferers, and at three o'clock in the afternoon had the pleasure of entering the fort, whence a party was sent the next morning with provisions. This party returned on the third day, bringing with it Lieutenant Jemette and the rest, in safety. Major Etherington, of the Sixtieth Regiment, who had arrived in the preceding autumn, now commanded at the fort.

I remained at Michilimackinac until the tenth of March, on which day I set out on my return to the Sault, taking the route of the Bay of Boutchitaouy [St. Martin Bay] which the ice had now rendered practicable. From the bottom of the bay the course lies in a direct line through the woods, a journey I performed in two days, though I was now troubled with a disorder, called the *snowshoe evil*, proceeding from an unusual strain on the tendons of the leg, occasioned by the weight of the snowshoe and which brings on inflammation. The remedy prescribed in the country is that of laying a piece of lighted touchwood on the part and leaving it there till the flesh is burnt to the nerve; but this experiment, though I had frequently seen it attended with success in others, I did not think proper to make upon myself.

The lands between the Bay of Boutchitaouy and the Sault are generally swampy, excepting so much of them as compose a ridge, or mountain, running east and west, and which is rocky and covered with the rock or sugar maple, or sugar wood, *(Acer saccharinum -Author)*. The season for making maple sugar was now at hand; and shortly after my arrival at the Sault I removed with the other inhabitants to the place at which we were to perform the manufacture.

A certain part of the maple woods having been chosen, and which was distant about three miles from the fort, a house twenty feet long and fourteen broad was begun in the morning, and before night made fit for the comfortable reception of eight persons and their baggage. It was open at top, had a door at each end, and a fireplace in the middle running the whole length.

The next day was employed in gathering the bark of white birch trees with which to make vessels to catch the wine or sap. The trees were now cut or tapped, and spouts or ducts introduced

Indian maple sugar camp drawn by Seth Eastman

into the wound. The bark vessels were placed under the ducts; and as they filled, the liquor was taken out in buckets and conveyed into reservoirs or vats of moose skin, each vat containing a hundred gallons. From these we supplied the boilers, of which we had twelve of from twelve to twenty gallons each, with fires constantly under them day and night. While the women collect the sap, boiled it, and completed the sugar, the men were not less busy in cutting wood, making fires, and in hunting and fishing in part of our supply of food.

The earlier part of the spring is that best adapted to making maple sugar. The sap runs only in the day; and it will not run unless there has been a frost the night before. When in the morning there is a clear sun and the night has left ice of the thickness of a dollar the greatest quantity is produced.

On the twenty-fifth of April our labor ended, and we returned to the fort, carrying with us as we found by the scales, sixteen hundred-weight of sugar. We had besides thirty-six gallons of syrup; and during our stay in the woods we certainly consumed three hundred-weight. Though, as I have said, we hunted and fished, yet sugar was our principal food during the whole month of April. I have known Indians to live wholly upon the same and become fat.

On the day of our return to the fort there arrived an English

gentleman, Sir Robert Davers, on a voyage of curiosity. I accompanied this gentleman on his return to Michilimackinac, which we reached on the twentieth of May.* My intention was to remain there till after my clerks should have come in from the interior, and then to go back to the Sault de Ste. Marie.

In the beginning of May the geese and ducks made their appearance, in their progress northward.

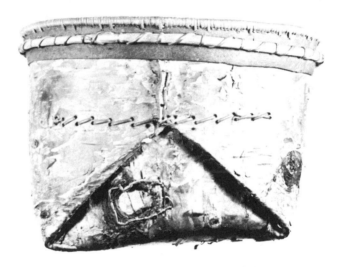

Indian birch bark container

8

The INDIANS
GROW RESTLESS

When I reached Michilimackinac I found several other traders who had arrived before me from different parts of the country, and who in general declared the dispositions of the Indians to be hostile to the English, and even apprehended some attack. M. Laurent Ducharme distinctly informed Major [George] Etherington [the Commandant] that a plan was absolutely conceived for destroying him, his garrison and all the English in the upper country; but the commandant, believing this and other reports to be without foundation, proceeding only from idle or ill-disposed persons, and of a tendency to do mischief, expressed much displeasure against M. Ducharme, and threatened to send the next person who should bring a story of the same kind a prisoner to Detroit.

The garrison at this time consisted of ninety privates, two subalterns and the commandant; and the English merchants at the fort were four in number.* Thus strong, few entertained anxiety concerning the Indians, who had no weapons but small arms.

Meanwhile the Indians from every quarter were daily assembling in unusual numbers, but with every appearance of friendship, frequenting the fort, and disposing of their peltries in such a manner as to dissipate almost every one's fears. For myself, on one occasion I took the liberty of observing to Major Etherington that in my judgment no confidence ought to be placed in them, and that I was informed no less than four hundred lay around the fort.

In return the Major only rallied me on my timidity; and it is to be confessed that if this officer neglected admonition on his part, so did I on mine. Shortly after my first arrival at Michilimackinac in the preceding year a Chippewa named Wawatam

---

*Actually the garrison only numbered thirty-five. The four merchants were Ezekiel Solomon, Henry Bostwick, Alexander Henry, and Mr. Tracy. -Editor.

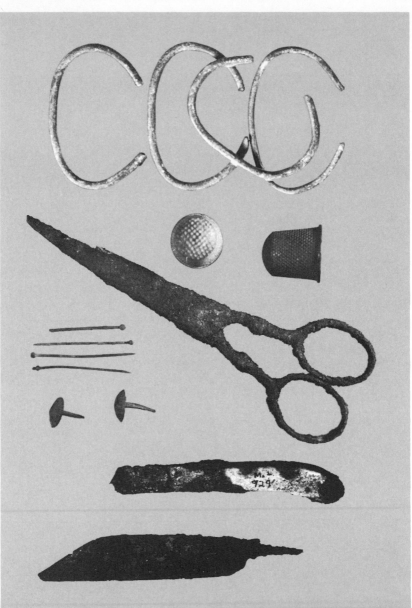

Items such as these Alexander Henry traded to the Indians in the 1760's. Found in recent years by Michigan State University archaeologists digging on the site of Fort Michilimackinac.

began to come often to my house, betraying in his demeanor strong marks of personal regard. After this had continued for some time he came on a certain day, bringing with him his whole family, and at the same time a large present, consisting of skins, sugar, and dried meat. Having laid these in a heap he commenced a speech in which he informed me that some years before he had observed a fast, devoting himself according to the custom of his nation to solitude and to the mortification of his body in the hope to obtain from the Great Spirit protection through all his days; that on this occasion he had dreamed of adopting an Englishman as his son, brother, and friend; that from the moment in which he first beheld me, he had recognized me as the person whom the Great Spirit had been pleased to point out to him for a brother; that he hoped that I would not refuse his present, and that he should forever regard me as one of his family.

I could do no otherwise than accept the present and declare my willingness to have so good a man as this appeared to be for my friend and brother. I offered a present in return for that which I had received, which Wawatam accepted, and then thanking me for the favor which he said that I had rendered him, he left me and soon after set out on his winter's hunt.

Twelve months had now elapsed since the occurrence of this incident, and I had almost forgotten the person of my *brother*, when on the second day of June, Wawatam came again to my house in a temper of mind visibly melancholy and thoughtful. He told me that he had just returned from his *wintering ground*, and I asked after his health; but without answering my question he went on to say that he was very sorry to find me returned from the Sault; that he had intended to go to that place himself immediately after his arrival at Michilimackinac; and that he wished me to go there, along with him and his family, the next morning. To all this he joined an inquiry whether or not the commandant had heard bad news, adding that during the winter he had himself been frequently disturbed with the *noise of evil birds*; and further suggesting that there were numerous Indians near the fort, many of whom had never shown themselves within it. Wawatam was about forty-five years of age, of an excellent character among his nation, and a chief.

Referring much of what I heard to the peculiarities of the Indian character, I did not pay all the attention which they will be found to have deserved to the entreaties and remarks of my visitor. I answered that I could not think of going to the Sault so soon as the next morning, but would follow him there after the arrival of my clerks. Finding himself unable to prevail with me he withdrew for that day; but early the next morning he came again, bringing with him his wife and a present of dried meat.

At this interview, after stating that he had several packs of beaver for which he intended to deal with me, he expressed a second time his apprehensions from the numerous Indians who were round the fort, and earnestly pressed me to consent to an immediate departure for the Sault. As a reason for this particular request he assured me that all the Indians proposed to come in a body that day to the fort to demand liquor of the commandant, and that he wished me to be gone before they should grow intoxicated.

I had made, at the period to which I am now referring, so much progress in the language in which Wawatam addressed me as to be able to hold an ordinary conversation in it; but the Indian manner of speech is so extravagantly figurative that it is only for a very perfect master to follow and comprehend it entirely. Had I been further advanced in this respect I think that I should have gathered so much information from this my friendly monitor as would have put me into possession of the design of the enemy, and enabled me to save as well others as myself; as it was, it unfortunately happened that I turned a deaf ear to everything, leaving Wawatam and his wife, after long and patient, but ineffectual efforts, to depart alone with dejected countenances, and not before they had each let fall some tears.

In the course of the same day I observed that the Indians came in great numbers into the fort, purchasing tomahawks (small axes of one pound weight) and frequently desiring to see silver arm bands and other valuable ornaments, of which I had a large quantity for sale. These ornaments, however, they in no instance purchased; but after turning them over, left them, saying that they would call again the next day. Their motive, as it afterward appeared, was no other than the very artful one of discovering, by requesting to see them, the particular places of their deposit so that they might lay their hands on them in the moment of pillage with the greater certainty and dispatch.

At night I turned in my mind the visits of Wawatam; but though they were calculated to excite uneasiness nothing induced me to believe that serious mischief was at hand. The next day being the fourth of June was the King's birthday.*

---

*Contemporary documents show that the attack occurred on June 2 instead of June 4. -Editor.

48

9
ATTACK

The morning was sultry. A Chippewa came to tell me that his nation was going to play at *baggatiway* with the Sacs or Saakies, another Indian nation, for a high wager. He invited me to witness the sport, adding that the commandant was to be there, and would bet on the side of the Chippewa. In consequence of this information I went to the commandant and expostulated with him a little, representing that the Indians might possibly have some sinister end in view; but the commandant only smiled at my suspicions.

Baggatiway, called by the Canadians *le jeu de la crosse*, is played with a bat and ball. The bat is about four feet in length, curved, and terminating in a sort of racket. Two posts are planted in the ground at a considerable distance from each other, as a mile or more. Each party has its post, and the game consists in throwing the ball up to the post of the adversary. The ball, at the beginning, is placed in the middle of the course and each party endeavors as well to throw the ball out of the direction of its own post as into that of the adversary's.

I did not go myself to see the match which was now to be played without the fort, because there being a canoe prepared to depart on the following day for Montreal I employed myself in writing letters to my friends; and even when a fellow trader, Mr. Tracy, happened to call upon me, saying that another canoe had just arrived from Detroit, and proposing that I should go with him to the beach to inquire the news, it so happened that I still remained to finish my letters, promising to follow Mr. Tracy in the course of a few minutes. Mr. Tracy had not gone more than twenty paces from my door when I heard an Indian war cry and a noise of general confusion.

Going instantly to my window I saw a crowd of Indians within the fort furiously cutting down and scalping every Englishman they found. In particular I witnessed the fate of Lieutenant Jemette.

Prelude to attack. Unsuspecting soldiers watch a vigorous baggatiway *game. —*
Courtesy of Michigan Bell Telephone Company

I had in the room in which I was a fowling piece, loaded with swanshot. This I immediately seized and held it for a few minutes, waiting to hear the drum beat to arms. In this dreadful interval I saw several of my countrymen fall, and more than one struggling between the knees of an Indian who, holding him in this manner, scalped him while yet living.

At length, disappointed in the hope of seeing resistance made to the enemy, and sensible, of course, that no effort of my own unassisted arm could avail against four hundred Indians, I thought only of seeking shelter. Amid the slaughter which was raging I observed many of the Canadian inhabitants of the fort calmly looking on, neither opposing the Indians, nor suffering injury; and from this circumstance I conceived a hope of finding security in their houses.

Between the yard door of my own house and that of M. [Charles] Langlade, my next neighbor, there was only a low fence, over which I easily climbed. At my entrance I found the whole family at the windows, gazing at the scene of blood before them. I addressed myself immediately to M. Langlade, begging that he would put me into some place of safety until the heat of the affair should be over; an act of charity by which he might perhaps preserve me from the general massacre; but while I uttered my petition, M. Langlade, who had looked for a moment at me, turned again to the window, shrugging his shoulders and intimating that he could do nothing for me: — *"Que voudriez-vous que j'en ferais?"* [What do you want me to do about it?]

This was a moment for despair; but the next a Pani woman,* a slave of M. Langlade's beckoned me to follow her. She brought me to a door which she opened, desiring me to enter, and telling me that it led to the garret, where I must go and conceal myself. I joyfully obeyed her directions; and she, having followed me up to the garret door, locked it after me and with great presence of mind took away the key.

This shelter obtained, if shelter I could hope to find it, I was naturally anxious to know what might still be passing without. Through an aperture which afforded me a view of the area of the fort I beheld, in shapes the foulest and most terrible, the ferocious triumphs of barbarian conquerors. The dead were scalped and mangled; the dying were writhing and shrieking under the unsatiated knife and tomahawk; and from the bodies of some, ripped open, their butchers were drinking the blood, scooped up in the hollow of joined hands and quaffed amid shouts of rage and victory. I was shaken not only with horror, but with fear. The sufferings which I witnessed I seemed on the point of ex-

---

*The Panies are an Indian nation of the south. -Author.

Reconstructed French trader's house and fort land gate, where Indian uprising started in June, 1763.

periencing. No long time elapsed before every one being destroyed who could be found, there was a general cry of "All is finished." At the same instant I heard some of the Indians enter the house in which I was.

The garret was separated from the room below only by a layer of single boards, at once the flooring of the one and the ceiling of the other. I could therefore hear everything that passed; and the Indians no sooner came in than they inquired whether or not any Englishman were in the house. M. Langlade replied that he could not say — he did not know of any — answers in which he did not exceed the truth, for the Pani woman had not only hidden me by stealth, but kept my secret and her own. M. Langlade was therefore, as I presume, as far from a wish to destroy me as he was careless about saving me, when he added to these answers that they might examine for themselves; and would soon be satisfied as to the object of their question. Saying this, he brought them to the garret door.

The state of my mind will be imagined. Arrived at the door some delay was occasioned by the absence of the key and a few moments were thus allowed me in which to look around for a hiding place. In one corner of the garret was a heap of those vessels of birch bark used in maple sugar making as I have recently described.

The door was unlocked, and opening, and the Indians ascending the stairs before I had completely crept into a small opening, which presented itself, at one end of the heap. An instant after, four Indians entered the room all armed with tomahawks, and all besmeared with blood, upon every part of their bodies.

The die appeared to be cast. I could scarcely breathe; but I thought that the throbbing of my heart occasioned a noise loud enough to betray me. The Indians walked in every direction about the garret, and one of them approached me so closely that at a particular moment, had he put forth his hand, he must have touched me. Still I remained undiscovered, a circumstance to which the dark color of my clothes and the want of light in a room which had no window, and in the corner in which I was, must have contributed. In a word, after taking several turns in the room, during which they told M. Langlade how many they had killed and how many scalps they had taken, they returned down stairs, and I with sensations not to be expressed, heard the door, which was the barrier between me and my fate, locked for the second time.

There was a feather bed on the floor, and on this, exhausted as I was by the agitation of my mind, I threw myself down and fell asleep. In this state I remained till the dusk of the evening, when I was awakened by a second opening of the door. The

Locks and keys from 1763 buildings found on fort site by archaeologists

person that now entered was M. Langlade's wife, who was much surprised at finding me, but advised me not to be uneasy, observing that the Indians had killed most of the English, but that she hoped I might myself escape. A shower of rain having begun to fall, she had come to stop a hole in the roof. On her going away, I begged her to send me a little water to drink, which she did.

As night was now advancing I continued to lie on the bed, ruminating on my condition, but unable to discover a resource from which I could hope for life. A flight to Detroit had no probable chance of success. The distance from Michilimackinac was four hundred miles; I was without provisions; and the whole length of the road lay through Indian countries, countries of an enemy in arms, where the first man whom I should meet would kill me. To stay where I was threatened nearly the same issue. As before, fatigue of mind, and not tranquillity, suspended my cares and procured me further sleep.

Reconstruction of Charles Langlade's house where Henry hid

Detail from diorama showing attack scene outside land gate

10

CAPTURE

The game of baggatiway, as from the description above will have been perceived, is necessarily attended with much violence and noise. In the ardor of contest the ball, as has been suggested, if it cannot be thrown to the goal desired, is struck in any direction by the adversary. At such a moment, therefore, nothing could be less liable to excite premature alarm than that the ball should be tossed over the pickets of the fort, nor that having fallen there, it should be followed on the instant by all engaged in the game, as well the one party as the other, all eager, all struggling, all shouting, all in the unrestrained pursuit of a rude athletic exercise. Nothing could be less fitted to excite premature alarm — nothing, therefore, could be more happily devised, under the circumstances, than a stratagem like this; and this was in fact the stratagem which the Indians had employed, by which they had obtained possession of the fort, and by which they had been enabled to slaughter and subdue its garrison and such of its other inhabitants as they pleased. To be still more certain of success they had prevailed upon as many as they could by a pretext the least liable to suspicion to come voluntarily without the pickets, and particularly the commandant and garrison themselves.

The respite which sleep afforded me during the night was put an end to by the return of morning. I was again on the rack of apprehension. At sunrise I heard the family stirring, and presently after, Indian voices informing M. Langlade they had not found my hapless self among the dead, and that they supposed me to be somewhere concealed. M. Langlade appeared from what followed to be by this time acquainted with the place of my retreat, of which no doubt he had been informed by his wife. The poor woman, as soon as the Indians mentioned me, declared to her husband in the French tongue that he should no longer keep me in his house, but deliver me up to my pursuers, giving as a reason for this measure that should the Indians discover his instrumentality in my concealment, they might revenge it on her children, and that it was better that I should die than they. M. Langlade resisted at first this sentence of his wife's; but soon suffered her to prevail, informing the Indians that he had been told I was in his house, that I had come there without his knowledge, and that he would put me into their hands. This was no sooner expressed than he began to ascend the stairs, the Indians following upon his heels.

I now resigned myself to the fate which I was menaced; and regarding every attempt at concealment as vain, I arose from the bed and presented myself full in view to the Indians who were entering the room. They were all in a state of intoxication, and entirely naked, except about the middle. One of them, named Wenniway, whom I had previously known, and who was upward of six feet in height, had his entire face and body covered with charcoal and grease, only that a white spot of two inches in diameter encircled either eye. This man, walking up to me, seized me with one hand by the collar of the coat, while in the other he held a large carving knife, as if to plunge it into my breast; his eyes, meanwhile, were fixed steadfastly on mine. At length, after some seconds of the most anxious suspense, he dropped his arm, saying, "I won't kill you." To this he added that he had been frequently engaged in wars against the English, and had brought away many scalps; that on a certain occasion he had lost a brother whose name was Musinigon, and that I should be called after him.

A reprieve upon any terms placed me among the living, and gave me back the sustaining voice of hope; but Wenniway ordered me downstairs, and there informing me that I was to be taken to his cabin, where, and indeed everywhere else, the Indians were all mad with liquor, death again was threatened, and not as possible only, but as certain. I mentioned my fears on this subject to M. Langlade, begging him to represent the danger to my master. M. Langlade in this instance did not withhold his compassion, and Wenniway immediately consented that I should remain where I was until he found another opportunity to take me away.

Thus far secure I reascended my garret stairs in order to place myself the furthest possible out of the reach of insult from drunken Indians; but I had not remained there more than an hour, when I was called to the room below in which was an Indian who said that I must go with him out of the fort, Wenniway having sent him to fetch me. This man, as well as Wenniway himself, I had seen before. In the preceding year I had allowed him to take goods on credit, for which he was still in my debt; and some short time previous to the surprise of the fort he had

Copper pail similar to those Henry traded in 1763

Breast plate gorget given to Indians by the British in the 18th century

said upon my upbraiding him with want of honesty that "He would pay me before long." This speech now came fresh into my memory and led me to suspect that the fellow had formed a design against my life. I communicated the suspicion to M. Langlade; but he gave for answer that "I was not now my own master, and must do as I was ordered."

The Indian on his part directed that before I left the house I should undress myself, declaring that my coat and shirt would become him better than they did me. His pleasure in this respect being complied with, no other alternative was left me than either to go out naked, or to put on the clothes of the Indian, which he freely gave me in exchange. His motive for this stripping me of my own apparel was no other as I afterward learned than this, that it might not be stained with blood when he should kill me.

I was now told to proceed; and my driver followed me close until I had passed the gate of the fort, when I turned toward the spot where I knew the Indians to be encamped. This, however, did not suit the purpose of my enemy, who seized me by the arm and drew me violently in the opposite direction to the distance of fifty yards above the fort. Here, finding that I was approaching the bushes and sand hills, I determined to proceed no farther, but told the Indian that I believed he meant to murder me, and that if so he might as well strike where I was as at any greater distance. He replied with coolness that my suspicions were just, and that he meant to pay me in this manner for my goods. At the same time he produced a knife and held me in a position to receive the intended blow. Both this and that which followed were necessarily the affair of a moment. By some effort, too sudden and too little dependent on thought to be explained or remembered, I was enabled to arrest his arm and give him a sudden push by which I turned him from me and released myself from his grasp. This was no sooner done than I ran toward the fort with all the swiftness in my power, the Indian following me, and I expecting every moment to feel his knife. I succeeded in my flight; and on entering the fort I saw Wenniway standing in the midst of the area, and to him I hastened for protection. Wenniway desired the Indian to desist; but the latter pursued me round him, making several strokes at me with his knife, and foaming at the mouth with rage at the repeated failure of his purpose. At length Wenniway drew near to M. Langlade's house; and the door being open, I ran into it. The Indian followed me; but on my entering the house he voluntarily abandoned the pursuit.

Preserved so often and so unexpectedly as it had now been my lot to be, I returned to my garret with a strong inclination to believe that through the will of an overruling power no Indian enemy could do me hurt; but new trials, as I believed, were at hand when at ten o'clock in the evening I was aroused from sleep and once more desired to descend the stairs. Not less, however, to my satisfaction than surprise, I was summoned only to meet Major Etherington, Mr. Bostwick, and Lieutenant Lesslie, who were in the room below.

These gentlemen had been taken prisoners while looking at the game without the fort and immediately stripped of all their clothes. They were now sent into the fort under the charge of Canadians, because, the Indians having resolved on getting drunk, the chiefs were apprehensive that they would be murdered if they continued in the camp. Lieutenant Jemette and seventy soldiers had been killed; and but twenty Englishmen, including soldiers, were still alive.* These were all within the fort, together with nearly three hundred Canadians *(Belonging to the canoes, etc. -Author)*.

These being our numbers, myself and others proposed to Major Etherington to make an effort for regaining possession of the fort and maintaining it against the Indians. The Jesuit missionary [Father du Jaunay] was consulted on the project; but he discouraged us by his representations, not only of the merciless treatment which he must expect from the Indians should they regain their superiority, but of the little dependence which was to be placed upon our Canadian auxiliaries. Thus the fort and prisoners remained in the hands of the Indians, though through the whole night the prisoners and whites were in actual possession, and they were without the gates.

That whole night, or the greater part of it, was passed in mutual condolence, and my fellow prisoners shared my garret. In the morning, being again called down, I found my master, Wenniway, and was desired to follow him. He led me to a small house within the fort, where in a narrow room and almost dark I found Mr. Ezekiel Solomons, an Englishman from Detroit, and a soldier, all prisoners. With these I remained in painful suspense as to the scene that was next to present itself till ten o'clock in the forenoon, when an Indian arrived, and presently marched us to the lakeside where a canoe appeared ready for departure, and in which we found that we were to embark.

Our voyage, full of doubt as it was, would have commenced immediately, but that one of the Indians who was to be of the party was absent. His arrival was to be waited for; and this occasioned a very long delay during which we were exposed to a

*Captain Etherington notified his commanding officer at Detroit on June 12, 1763 that sixteen soldiers as well as the trader Mr. Tracy had been killed and two soldiers wounded in the massacre. Since that time five of those taken prisoner had also been killed. - Editor.

keen northeast wind. An old shirt was all that covered me; I suffered much from the cold; and in this extremity M. Langlade coming down to the beach, I asked him for a blanket, promising if I lived to pay him for it at any price he pleased; but the answer I received was this, that he could let me have no blanket unless there were some one to be security for the payment. For myself, he observed, I had no longer any property in that country. I had no more to say to M. Langlade; but presently seeing another Canadian, named John Cuchoise, I addressed to him a similar request and was not refused. Naked as I was, and rigorous as was the weather, but for the blanket I must have perished. At noon our party was all collected, the prisoners all embarked, and we steered for the Isles du Castor [Beaver Islands] in Lake Michigan.

The reconstructed water gate through which passed the military supplies and Indian trade materials

11

A CAPTIVE STILL

The soldier who was our companion in misfortune was made fast to a bar of the canoe by a rope tied round his neck, as is the manner of the Indians in transporting their prisoners. The rest were left unconfined; but a paddle was put into each of our hands and we were made to use it. The Indians in the canoe were seven in number, the prisoners four. I had left, as it will be recollected, Major Etherington, Lieutenant Lesslie, and Mr. Bostwick at M. Langlade's, and was now joined in misery with Mr. Ezekiel Solomons, the soldier, and the Englishman who had newly arrived from Detroit. This was on the sixth day of June. The fort was taken on the fourth; I surrendered myself to Wenniway on the fifth; and this was the third day of our distress.

We were bound, as I have said, for the Isles du Castor which lie in the mouth of Lake Michigan; and we should have crossed the lake, but that a thick fog came on, on account of which the Indians deemed it safer to keep the shore close under their lee. We therefore approached the lands of the Ottawa and their village of L'Arbre Croche already mentioned as lying about twenty miles to the westward of Michilimackinac on the opposite side of the tongue of land on which the fort is built.

Every half hour the Indians gave their war whoops, one for every prisoner in their canoe. This is a general custom, by the aid of which all other Indians within hearing are apprised of the number of prisoners they are carrying.

In this manner we reached Wagoshense *(Fox Point -Author)**, a long point stretching westward into the lake and which the Ottawa make a carrying place to avoid going round it. It is distant eighteen miles from Michilimackinac. After the Indians had made their war whoop as before an Ottawa appeared upon

---

*A few miles west of Wilderness State Park. -Editor.

the beach, who made signs that we should land. In consequence
we approached. The Ottawa asked the news and kept the Chippewa in further conversation till we were within a few yards of
land and in shallow water. At this moment a hundred men rushed
upon us from among the bushes and dragged all the prisoners
out of the canoes amid a terrifying shout.

We now believed that our last sufferings were approaching;
but no sooner were we fairly on shore and on our legs than the
chiefs of the party advanced and gave each of us their hands,
telling us that they were our friends, and Ottawa, whom the
Chippewa had insulted by destroying the English without consulting with them on the affair. They added that what they had
done was for the purpose of saving our lives, the Chippewa having been carrying us to the Isles du Castro only to kill and
devour us.

The reader's imagination is here distracted by the variety of
our fortunes, and he may well paint to himself the state of mind
of those who sustained them; who were the sport, or the victims,
of a series of events more like dreams than realities, more like
fiction than truth. It was not long before we were embarked again
in the canoes of the Ottawa, who, the same evening, re-landed us
at Michilimackinac, where they marched us into the fort in view
of the Chippewa, confounded at beholding the Ottawa espouse a
side opposite their own.

The Ottawa, who had accompanied us in sufficient numbers, took possession of the fort. We, who had changed masters but were still prisoners, were lodged in the house of the commandant and strictly guarded.

Early the next morning a general council was held, in which the Chippewa complained much of the conduct of the Ottawa in robbing them of their prisoners, alleging that all the Indians, the Ottawa alone excepted, were at war with the English; that Pontiac had taken Detroit; that the King of France had awoke, and repossessed himself of Quebec and Montreal; and that the English were meeting destruction, not only at Michilimackinac, but in every other part of the world. From all this they inferred that it became the Ottawa to restore the prisoners and to join in the war; and the speech was followed by large presents; being part of the plunder of the fort, and which was previously heaped in the center of the room. The Indians rarely make their answers till the day after they have heard the arguments offered. They did not depart from their custom on this occasion, and the council therefore adjourned.

We, the prisoners, whose fate was thus in controversy, were unacquainted at the time with this transaction, and therefore enjoyed a night of tolerable tranquillity, not in the least suspecting

*Henry captured and
taken to the Beaver Islands*

the reverse which was preparing for us. Which of the arguments of the Chippewa, or whether or not all were deemed valid by the Ottawa, I cannot say; but the council was resumed at an early hour in the morning and after several speeches had been made in it the prisoners were sent for and returned to the Chippewa.

The Ottawa, who now gave us into the hands of the Chippewa, had themselves declared that the latter designed no other than to kill us and *make broth of us*. The Chippewa, as soon as we were restored to them, marched us to a village of their own, situate on the point which is below the fort, and put us into a lodge already the prison of fourteen soldiers, tied two and two, with each a rope about his neck, and made fast to a pole which might be called the supporter of the building.

I was left untied; but I passed a night sleepless and full of wretchedness. My bed was the bare ground, and I was again reduced to an old shirt as my entire apparel; the blanket which I had received through the generosity of M. Cuchoise having been taken from me among the Ottawa when they seized upon myself and the others at Wagoshense. I was, besides, in want of food, having for two days ate nothing.

I confess that in the canoe with the Chippewa I was offered bread — but bread with what accompaniment. They had a loaf which they cut with the same knives that they had employed in the massacre — knives still covered with blood. The blood they moistened with spittle, and rubbing it on the bread offered this for food to their prisoners, telling them to eat the blood of their countrymen.

Such was my situation on the morning of the seventh of June, in the year one thousand seven hundred and sixty-three; but a few hours produced an event which gave still a new color to my lot.

Toward noon, when the great war chief, in company with Wenniway, was seated at the opposite end of the lodge, my friend and brother, Wawatam, suddenly came in. During the four days preceding I had often wondered what had become of him. In passing by he gave me his hand, but went immediately toward the great chief by the side of whom and Wenniway he sat himself down. The most uninterrupted silence prevailed; each smoked his pipe; and this done, Wawatam arose and left the lodge, saying to me as he passed, "Take courage."

12
BEFRIENDED
by
WAWATAM

An hour elapsed, during which several chiefs entered and preparations appeared to be making for a council. At length Wawatam re-entered the lodge, followed by his wife, and both loaded with merchandise which they carried up to the chiefs and laid in a heap before them. Some moments of silence followed, at the end of which Wawatam pronounced a speech, every word of which to me was of extraordinary interest:

"Friends and relations," he began, "what is it that I shall say? You know what I feel. You all have friends and brothers and children, whom as yourselves you love; and you—what would you experience, did you, like me behold your dearest friend —your brother—in the condition of a slave; a slave, exposed every moment to insult, and to menaces of death? This case, as you all know, is mine. See there *(pointing to myself)* my friend and brother among slaves—himself a slave.

"You all well know that long before the war began I adopted him as my brother. From that moment he became one of my family, so that no change of circumstances could break the cord which fastened us together.

"He is my brother; and because I am your relation he is therefore your relation, too:—and how, being your relation, can he be your slave?

"On the day on which the war began you were fearful lest on this very account I should reveal your secret. You requested, therefore, that I would leave the fort, and even cross the lake. I did so; but I did it with reluctance. I did it with reluctance, notwithstanding that you, Menehwehna, who had the command in this enterprise, gave me your promise that you would protect my friend, delivering him from all danger, and giving him safely to me.

"The performance of this promise I now claim. I come not

with empty hands to ask it. You, Menehwehna, best know whether or not, as it respects yourself, you have kept your word, but I bring these goods to buy off every claim which any man among you all may have on my brother, as his prisoner.''

Wawatam having ceased, the pipes were again filled; and after they were finished a further period of silence followed. At the end of this, Menehwehna arose and gave his reply:

"My relation and brother," said he, "what you have spoken is the truth. We were acquainted with the friendship which subsisted between yourself and the Englishman in whose behalf ̣ou have now addressed us. We knew the danger of having our secret discovered, and the consequences which must follow; and you say truly that we requested you to leave the fort. This we did out of regard for you and your family; for if a discovery of our design had been made, you would have been blamed, whether guilty or not; and you would thus have been involved in difficulties from which you could not have extricated yourself.

"It is also true that I promised you to take care of your friend; and this promise I performed by desiring my son, at the moment of assault, to seek him out and bring him to my lodge. He went accordingly, but could not find him. The day after I sent him to Langlade's, when he was informed that your friend was safe; and had it not been that the Indians were then drinking the rum which had been found in the fort he would have brought him home with him, according to my orders.

"I am very glad to find that your friend has escaped. We accept your present; and you may take him home with you."

Wawatam thanked the assembled chiefs, and taking me by the hand, led me to his lodge, which was at the distance of a few yards only from the prison lodge. My entrance appeared to give joy to the whole family; food was immediately prepared for me; and I now ate the first hearty meal which I had made since my capture. I found myself one of the family; and but that I had still my fears as to the other Indians I felt as happy as the situation could allow.

In the course of the next morning I was alarmed by a noise in the prison lodge; and looking through the opening of the lodge in which I was, I saw seven dead bodies of white men dragged forth. Upon my inquiry into the occasion I was informed that a certain chief called by the Canadians Le Grand Sable had not long before arrived from his winter's hunt; and that he, having been absent when the war begun, and being now desirous of manifesting to the Indians at large his hearty concurrence in what they had done, had gone into the prison lodge, and there, with his knife, put the seven men, whose bodies I had seen, to death.

Shortly after two of the Indians took one of the dead bodies which they chose as being the fattest, cut off the head, and divided the whole into five parts, one of which was put into each of five kettles, hung over as many fires kindled for this purpose at the door of the prison lodge. Soon after things were so far prepared a message came to our lodge with an invitation to Wawatam to assist at the feast.

An invitation to a feast is given by him who is the master of it. Small cuttings of cedar wood, of about four inches in length, supply the place of cards; and the bearer, by word of mouth, states the particulars.

Wawatam obeyed the summons, taking with him as is usual to the place of entertainment his dish and spoon.

After an absence of about half an hour he returned bringing in his dish a human hand and a large piece of flesh. He did not appear to relish the repast, but told me that it was then and always had been the custom among all the Indian nations when returning from war, or on overcoming their enemies, to make a war feast from among the slain. This, he said, inspired the warrior with courage in attack, and bred him to meet death with fearlessness.

In the evening of the same day a large canoe, such as those which came from Montreal, was seen advancing to the fort. It was full of men, and I distinguished several passengers. The Indian cry was made in the village; a general muster ordered; and, to the number of two hundred, they marched up to the fort where the canoe was expected to land. The canoe, suspecting nothing, came boldly to the fort, where the passengers, as being English traders, were seized, dragged through the water, beat, reviled, marched to the prison lodge, and there stripped of their clothes, and confined.

Of the English traders that fell into the hands of the Indians at the capture of the fort, Mr. Tracy was the only one who lost his life. Mr. Ezekiel Solomons and Mr. Henry Bostwick were taken by the Ottawa, and after the peace, carried down to Montreal, and there ransomed. Of ninety troops about seventy were killed; the rest, together with those of the posts in the Bay des Puants [Green Bay], and at the River St. Joseph, were also kept in safety by the Ottawa till the peace, and then either freely restored, or ransomed at Montreal.* The Ottawa never overcame

---

*The garrison at Green Bay, summoned by Captain Etherington to join him at L'Arbre Croche, was escorted across Lake Michigan by a band of friendly Menominee. The garrison at St. Joseph was massacred on May 25 by the Potawatomi and the four survivors were taken to Detroit where they were exchanged for certain Indians held by the beseiged garrison. -Editor.

their disgust at the neglect with which they had been treated in the beginning of the war by those who afterward desired their assistance as allies.

Pipe tomahawk from Michilimackinac. — Courtesy of City of Liverpool Museums

13

SKULL CAVE

In the morning of the ninth of June a general council was held, at which it was agreed to remove to the island of Michilimackinac, as a more defensible situation, in the event of an attack by the English. The Indians had begun to entertain apprehensions of want of strength. No news had reached them from the Potawatomi, in the Bay des Puants; and they were uncertain whether or not the Monomins* would join them. They even feared that the Sioux would take the English side.

This resolution fixed, they prepared for a speedy retreat. At noon the camp was broken up, and we embarked, taking with us the prisoners that were still undisposed of. On our passage we encountered a gale of wind, and there were some appearances of danger. To avert it, a dog, of which the legs were previously tied together, was thrown into the lake; an offering designed to soothe the angry passions of some offended Manito.

As we approached the island two women in the canoe in which I was began to utter melancholy and hideous cries. Precarious as my condition still remained I experienced some sensations of alarm from these dismal sounds, of which I could not then discover the occasion. Subsequently I learned that it is customary for the women on passing near the burial places of relations never to omit the practice of which I was now a witness, and by which they intend to denote their grief.

By the approach of evening we reached the island in safety, and the women were not long in erecting our cabins. In the morning there was a muster of the Indians, at which there were found three hundred and fifty fighting men.

*Manomines or Malomines. In the first syllable the substitution of l for n, and n for l, marks one of the differences in the Chippewa and Algonquin dialects. In the mouth of an Algonquin it is *Michilimackinac*; in that of a Chippewa, *Michinimackinac*. -Author.

71

In the course of the day there arrived a canoe from Detroit, with ambassadors, who endeavored to prevail on the Indians to repair thither to the assistance of Pontiac; but fear was now the prevailing passion. A guard was kept during the day and a watch by night, and alarms were very frequently spread. Had an enemy appeared all the prisoners would have been put to death; and I suspected that as an Englishman I should share their fate.

Several days had not passed, when one morning a continued alarm prevailed, and I saw the Indians running in a confused manner toward the beach. In a short time I learned that two large canoes from Montreal were in sight.

All the Indian canoes were immediately manned, and those from Montreal were surrounded and seized as they turned the point behind which the flotilla had been concealed. The goods were consigned to a Mr. Levy, and would have been saved if the canoe men had called them French property; but they were terrified, and disguised nothing.

In the canoes was a large proportion of liquor, a dangerous acquisition, and which threatened disturbance among the Indians, even to the loss of their dearest friends. Wawatam, always watchful of my safety, no sooner heard the noise of drunkenness, which in the evening did not fail to begin, than he represented to me the danger of remaining in the village, and owned that he could not himself resist the temptation of joining his comrades in the debauch. That I might escape all mischief, he, therefore, requested that I would accompany him to the mountain, where I was to remain hidden till the liquor should be drunk.

We ascended the mountain accordingly. It is this mountain which constitutes that high land in the middle of the island, of which I have spoken before, as of a figure considered as resembling a *turtle*, and therefore called *michilimackinac*. It is thickly covered with wood, and very rocky toward the top. After walking more than half a mile we came to a large rock at the base of which was an opening, dark within, appearing to be the entrance of a cave.

Here Wawatam recommended that I should take up my lodging, and by all means to remain till he returned.

On going into the cave, of which the entrance was nearly ten feet wide, I found the farther end to be rounded in its shape, like that of an oven but with a further aperture, too small, however to be explored.

After thus looking around me I broke small branches from the trees and spread them for a bed; then wrapped myself in my blanket, and slept till daybreak.

On awakening I felt myself incommoded by some object upon which I lay; and removing it found it to be a bone. This

I supposed to be that of a deer, or some other animal, and what might very naturally be looked for in the place in which I was; but when daylight visited my chamber I discovered with feelings of horror that I was lying on nothing less than a heap of human bones and skulls which covered all the floor.

The day passed without the return of Wawatam, and without food. As night approached I found myself unable to meet its darkness in the charnel house, which, nevertheless, I had viewed free from uneasiness during the day. I chose, therefore, an adjacent bush for this night's lodging, and slept under it as before; but in the morning I awoke hungry and dispirited, and almost envying the dry bones, to the view of which I returned. At length the sound of a foot reached me, and my Indian friend appeared, making many apologies for his long absence, the cause of which was an unfortunate excess in the enjoyment of his liquor.

This point being explained, I mentioned the extraordinary sight that had presented itself in the cave to which he had commended my slumbers. He had never heard of its existence before; and upon examining the cave together we saw reason to believe that it had been anciently filled with human bodies.

On returning to the lodge I experienced a cordial reception from the family, which consisted of the wife of my friend, his two sons, of whom the eldest was married, and whose wife and a daughter of thirteen years of age, completed the list.

Wawatam related to the other Indians the adventure of the bones. All of them expressed surprise at hearing it, and declared that they had never been aware of the contents of this cave before. After visiting it, which they immediately did, almost every one offered a different opinion as to its history.

Some advanced that at a period when the waters overflowed the land (an event which makes a distinguished figure in the history of their world) the inhabitants of this island had fled into the cave, and been there drowned; others, that those same inhabitants, when the Hurons made war upon them (as tradition says they did) hid themselves in the cave, and being discovered, were there massacred. For myself, I am disposed to believe that this cave was an ancient receptacle for the bones of prisoners sacrificed and devoured at war feasts. I have always observed that the Indians pay particular attention to the bones of sacrifices, preserving them unbroken, and depositing them in some place kept exclusively for that purpose.

Chippewa Indian cradle board for carrying papoose

14
INDIAN
MEDICINE

A few days after the occurrence of the incidents recorded in the preceding chapter, Menehwehna, whom I now found to be the great chief of the village of Michilimackinac, came to the lodge of my friend; and when the usual ceremony of smoking was finished, he observed that Indians were now daily arriving from Detroit, some of whom had lost relations or friends in the war, and who would certainly retaliate on any Englishman they found; upon which account his errand was to advise that I should be dressed like an Indian, an expedient whence I might hope to escape all future insult.

I could not but consent to the proposal, and the chief was so kind as to assist my friend and his family in effecting that very day the desired metamorphosis. My hair was cut off, and my head shaved with the exception of a spot on the crown of about twice the diameter of a crown-piece. My face was painted with three or four different colors, some parts of it red, and others black. A shirt was provided for me, painted with vermilion mixed with grease. A large collar of wampum was put round my neck, and another suspended on my breast. Both my arms were decorated with large bands of silver above the elbows, besides several smaller ones on the wrists; and my legs were covered with *mitases*, a kind of hose made, as is the favorite fashion, of scarlet cloth. Over all I was to wear a scarlet blanket or mantle, and on my head a large bunch of feathers. I parted, not without some regret, with the long hair which was natural to it and which I fancied to be ornamental; but the ladies of the family and of the village in general appeared to think my person improved, and now condescended to call me handsome, even among Indians.

Protected in a great measure by this disguise, I felt myself more at liberty than before; and the season being arrived in which my clerks from the interior were to be expected and some part of my property, as I had a right to hope, recovered, I begged the favor of Wawatam that he would enable me to pay a short visit to Michilimackinac. He did not fail to comply, and I succeeded in finding my clerks; but, either through the disturbed state of the country, as they represented to be the case, or through their misconduct, as I had reason to think, I obtained nothing; and nothing or almost nothing, I now began to think, would be all that I should need during the rest of my life. To fish and to hunt, to collect a few skins, and exchange them for necessaries, was all that I seemed destined to do and to acquire for the future.

I returned to the Indian village where at this time much scarcity of food prevailed. We were often for twenty-four hours without eating; and when in the morning we had no victuals for the day before us the custom was to black our faces with grease and charcoal, and exhibit through resignation a temper as cheerful as if in the midst of plenty.

A repetition of the evil, however, soon induced us to leave the island in search of food; and accordingly we departed for the Bay of Boutchitaouy, distant eight leagues, and where we found plenty of wild fowl and fish.

While in the bay my guardian's daughter-in-law was taken in labor of her first child. She was immediately removed out of the common lodge; and a small one for her separate accommodation was begun and finished by the women in less than half an hour.

The next morning we heard that she was very ill, and the family began to be much alarmed on her account; the more so, no doubt, because cases of difficult labor are very rare among Indian women. In this distress, Wawatam requested me to accompany him into the woods; and on our way informed me that if he could find a snake he should soon secure relief to his daughter-in-law.

On reaching some wet ground we speedily obtained the object of our search in a small snake of the kind called the garter snake. Wawatam seized it by the neck; and holding it fast while it coiled itself around his arm, he cut off its head, catching the blood in a cup that he had brought with him. This done, he threw away the snake, and carried home the blood, which he mixed with a quantity of water. Of this mixture he administered first one table-spoonful, and shortly afterwards a second. Within an hour the patient was safely delivered of a fine child: and Wawatam subsequently declared that the remedy to which he had resorted was one that never failed.

On the next day we left the Bay of Boutchitaouy; and the young mother, in high spirits, assisted in loading the canoe, bare-footed, and knee deep in water.

The medical information, the diseases and the remedies of

76

the Indians often engaged my curiosity during the period through which I was familiar with these nations; and I shall take this occasion to introduce a few particulars connected with their history.

The Indians are in general free from disorders; and an instance of their being subject to dropsy, gout, or stone, never came within my knowledge. Inflammations of the lungs are among their most ordinary complaints, and rheumatism still more so, especially with the aged. Their mode of life, in which they are so much exposed to the wet and cold, sleeping on the ground, and inhaling the night air, sufficiently accounts for their liability to these diseases. The remedies on which they most rely are emetics, cathartics, and the lancet; but especially the last. Bleeding is so favorite an operation among the women that they never lose an occasion of enjoying it, whether sick or well. I have sometimes bled a dozen women in a morning as they sat in a row along a fallen tree, beginning with the first — opening the vein — then proceeding to the second — and so on, having three or four individuals bleeding at the same time.

In most villages, and particularly in those of the Chippewa, this service was required of me; and no persuasion of mine could ever induce a woman to dispense with it.

In all parts of the country and among all the nations that I have seen, particular individuals arrogate to themselves the art of healing, but principally by means of pretended sorcery; and operations of this sort are always paid for by a present, made before they are begun. Indeed, whatever, as an impostor, may be the demerits of the operator, his reward may generally be said to be fairly earned by dint of corporal labor.

I was once present at a performance of this kind in which the patient was a female child of about twelve years of age. Several of the elder chiefs were invited to the scene; and the same compliment was paid to myself on account of the medical skill for which it was pleased to give me credit.

The physician (so to call him) seated himself on the ground; and before him on a new stroud blanket was placed a basin of water in which were three bones, the larger ones, as it appeared to me, of a swan's wing. In his hand he had his *shishiquoi*, or rattle, with which he beat time to his *medicine-song*. The sick child lay on a blanket near the physician. She appeared to have much fever, and a severe oppression of the lungs, breathing with difficulty, and betraying symptoms of the last stage of consumption.

After singing for some time the physician took one of the bones out of the basin: the bone was hollow; and one end being applied to the breast of the patient, he put the other into his mouth in order to remove the disorder by suction. Having persevered in this as long as he thought proper, he suddenly seemed to force the bone into his mouth and swallow it. He now acted the part of one suffering severe pain; but presently finding relief, he made a long speech, and after this returned to singing, and to the accompaniment of his rattle. With the latter, during his song, he struck his head, breast, sides and back; at the same time straining as if to vomit forth the bone.

Relinquishing this attempt, he applied himself to suction a second time, and with the second of the three bones; and this also he soon seemed to swallow.

Upon its disappearance he began to distort himself in the most frightful manner, using every gesture which could convey the idea of pain; at length he succeeded, or pretended to succeed, in throwing up one of the bones. This was handed about to the spectators, and strictly examined; but nothing remarkable could be discovered. Upon this he went back to his song and rattle: and after some time threw up the second of the two bones. In the groove of this the physician, upon examination, found and displayed to all present a small white substance, resembling a piece of the quill of a feather. It was passed round the company from one to the other; and declared by the physician to be the thing causing the disorder of his patient.

The multitude believe that these physicians, whom the French call *jongleurs*, or jugglers, can inflict as well as remove disorders. They believe that by drawing the figure of any person in sand or ashes, or on clay, or by considering any object as the figure of a person and then pricking it with a sharp stick or other substance, or doing in any other manner that which done to a living body would cause pain, or injury, the individual represented, or supposed to be represented, will suffer accordingly. On the other hand the mischief being done, another physician of equal pretension can by suction remove it. Unfortunately, however, the operations which I have described were not successful in the instance referred to; for on the day after they had taken place the girl died.

With regard to flesh wounds the Indians certainly effect astonishing cures. Here, as above, much that is fantastic occurs, but the success of their practice evinces something solid.

At the Sault de Ste. Marie I knew a man who in the result of a quarrel received the stroke of an axe in his side. The blow was so violent and the axe driven so deep that the wretch who held it could not withdraw it, but left it in the wound and fled. Shortly after the man was found and brought in to the fort where several other Indians came to his assistance. Among these, one, who was a physician, immediately withdrew in order to fetch his *penegusan*, or medicine bag, with which he soon returned. The eyes of the sufferer were fixed, his teeth closed, and his case apparently desperate.

The physician took from his bag a small portion of a very white sustance, resembling that of a bone; this he scraped into a little water and forcing open the jaws of the patient with a stick he poured the mixture down his throat. What followed was that in a very short space of time the wounded man moved his eyes, and beginning to vomit threw up a small lump of clotted blood.

The physician now, and not before, examined the wound from which I could see the breath escape, and from which a part of the omentum depended. This the physician did not set about to restore to its place; but cutting it away, minced it into small pieces and made his patient swallow it.

The man was then carried to his lodge where I visited him daily. By the sixth day he was able to walk about; and within a month he grew quite well except that he was troubled with a cough. Twenty years after his misfortune he was still alive.

Another man, being on his wintering ground and hunting beaver, was crossing a lake covered with smooth ice with two beavers on his back, when his foot slipped and he fell. At his side in his belt was his axe, the blade of which came upon the joint of his wrist; and the weight of his body coming upon the blade, his hand was completely separated from his arm with the exception of a small piece of the skin. He had to walk three miles to his lodge which was thus far away. The skin, which alone retained his hand to his arm, he cut through with the same axe which had done the rest; and fortunately having on a shirt, he took it off, tore it up, and made a strong ligature above the wrist, so as in some measure to avoid the loss of blood. On reaching his lodge he cured the wound himself by the mere use of simples. I was a witness to its perfect healing.

I have said that these physicians, jugglers, or practitioners of pretended sorcery, are supposed to be capable of inflicting diseases; and I may add that they are sometimes themselves sufferers on this account. In one instance I saw one of them killed by a man who charged him with having brought his brother to death by malefic arts. The accuser in his rage thrust his knife into the belly of the accused and ripped it open. The latter caught his bowels in his arms and thus walked toward his lodge, gathering them up from time to time as they escaped his hold. His lodge was at no considerable distance and he reached it alive and died in it.

15
WINTER
at
AUX SABLES

Our next encampment was on the Island of Saint Martin, off Cape St. Ignace, so called from the Jesuit mission of St. Ignatius to the Hurons formerly established there. Our object was to fish for sturgeon, which we did with great success; and here in the enjoyment of a plentiful and excellent supply of food we remained until the twentieth day of August. At this time, the autumn being at hand, and a sure prospect of increased security from hostile Indians afforded, Wawatam proposed going to his intended wintering ground. The removal was a subject of the greatest joy to myself on account of the frequent insults to which I had still to submit from the Indians of our band or village; and to escape from which I would freely have gone almost anywhere. At our wintering ground we were to be alone; for the Indian families in the countries of which I write separate in the winter season for the convenience as well of subsistence as of the chase, and re-associate in the spring and summer.

In preparation our first business was to sail for Michilimackinac, where, being arrived, we procured from a Canadian trader on credit some trifling articles together with ammunition and two bushels of maize. This done we steered directly for Lake Michigan. At L'Arbre Croche we stopped one day on a visit to the Ottawas where all the people, and particularly Okinochumaki, the chief, the same who took me from the Chippewa, behaved with great civility and kindness. The chief presented me with a bag of maize. It is the Ottawa, it will be remembered, who raise this grain for the market of Michilimackinac.

Leaving L'Arbre Croche, we proceeded direct to the mouth of the River Aux Sables* on the south side of the lake and dis-

*The exact identification of the River Aux Sables is uncertain but Henry apparently wintered in the vicinity of present day Ludington, Michigan. -Editor.

tant about a hundred and fifty miles from Fort Michilimackinac. On our voyage we passed several deep bays and rivers, and I found the banks of the lake to consist in mere sands without any appearance of verdure, the sand drifting from one hill to another like snow in winter. Hence all the rivers which here entered the lake are as much entitled to the epithet of sandy as that to which we were bound. They are also distinguished by another particularity always observable in similar situations. The current of the stream being met when the wind is contrary by the waves of the lake, it is driven back, and the sands of the shore are at the same time washed into its mouth. In consequence the river is able to force a passage into the lake, broad only in proportion to its utmost strength; while it hollows for itself behind the sandbanks a basin of one, two, or three miles across. In these rivers we killed many wild fowl and beaver.

To kill beaver we used to go several miles up the rivers before the approach of night, and after the dusk came on, suffer the canoe to drift gently down the current without noise. The beaver in this part of the evening come abroad to procure food or materials for repairing their habitations; and as they are not alarmed by the canoe, they often pass it within gun shot.

While we thus hunted along our way I enjoyed a personal freedom of which I had been long deprived, and became as expert in the Indian pursuits as the Indians themselves.

On entering the River Aux Sables, Wawatam took a dog, tied its feet together, and threw it into the stream, uttering at the same time a long prayer which he addressed to the Great Spirit, supplicating his blessing on the chase, and his aid in the support of the family through the dangers of a long winter. Our lodge was fifteen miles above the mouth of the stream. The principal animals which the country afforded were the stag, or red deer, the common American deer, the bear, raccoon, beaver, and marten.

The beaver feeds in preference on young wood of the birch, aspen, and poplar tree* but in defect of these, on any other tree, those of the pine and fir kinds excepted. These latter it employs only for building its dams and houses. In wide meadows where no wood is to be found it resorts for all its purposes to the roots of the rush and water lily. It consumes great quantities of food, whether of roots or wood; and hence often reduces itself to the necessity of removing into a new quarter. Its house has an arched dome-like roof, of an elliptical figure, and rises from three to four feet above the surface of the water. It is always entirely surrounded by water; but in the banks adjacent the animal pro-

---

*Populus nigra, called by the Canadians, liard. -Author.

vides holes or washes, of which the entrance is below the surface, and to which it retreats on the first alarm.

The female beaver usually produces two young at a time, but not infrequently more. During the first year the young remain with their parents. In the second, they occupy an adjoining apartment and assist in building and in procuring food. At two years old they part and build houses of their own, but often rove about for a considerable time before they fix upon a spot. There are beavers called by the Indians *old bachelors*, who live by themselves, build no houses, and work at no dams, but shelter themselves in holes. The usual method of taking these is by traps, formed of iron or logs, and baited with branches of poplar.

According to the Indians, the beaver is much given to jealousy. If a strange male approaches the cabin a battle immediately ensues. Of this the female remains an unconcerned spectator, careless to which party the law of conquest may assign her. Among the beaver which we killed, those who were with me pretended to show demonstrations of this fact, some of the skins of the males, and almost all of the older ones, bearing marks of violence, while none were ever to be seen on the skins of the females.

The Indians add that the male is as constant as he is jealous, never attaching himself to more than one female; while the female on her side is always fond of strangers.

The most common way of taking the beaver is that of breaking up its house,. which is done with trenching tools during the winter, when the ice is strong enough to allow of approaching them and when, also, the fur is in its most valuable state.

Breaking up the house, however, is only a preparatory step. During this operation the family made their escape to one or more of their *washes*. These are to be discovered by striking the ice along the bank, and where the holes are a hollow sound is returned. After discovering and searching many of these in vain we often found the whole family together in the same wash. I was taught occasionally to distinguish a full wash from an empty one by the motion of the water above its entrance occasioned by the breathing of the animals concealed in it. From the washes they must be taken out with the hands; and in doing this the hunter sometimes received severe wounds from their teeth. While a hunter, I thought with the Indians that the beaver flesh was very good; but after that of the ox was again within my reach I could not relish it. The tail is accounted a luxurious morsel.

Beavers, say the Indians, were formerly a people endowed with speech, not less than with the other noble faculties they possess; but the Great Spirit has taken this away from them lest they should grow superior in understanding to mankind.

The raccoon was another object of our chase. It was my

practice to go out in the evening with dogs, accompanied by the youngest son of my guardian, to hunt this animal. The raccoon never leaves its hiding place till after sunset.

As soon as a dog falls on a fresh track of the raccoon, he gives notice by a cry and immediately pursues. His barking enables the hunter to follow. The raccoon, which travels slowly and is soon overtaken, makes for a tree on which he remains till shot.

After the falling of the snow nothing more is necessary for taking the raccoon than to follow the track of his feet. In this season he seldom leaves his habitation; and he never lays up any food. I have found six at a time in the hollow of one tree lying upon each other, and nearly in a torpid state. In more than one instance I have ascertained that they have lived six weeks without food. The mouse is their principal prey.

Raccoon hunting was my more particular and daily employ. I usually went out at the first dawn of day and seldom returned till sunset, or till I had laden myself with as many animals as I could carry. By degrees I became familiarized with this kind of life; and had it not been for the idea of which I could not divest my mind, that I was living among savages, and for the whispers of a lingering hope that I should one day be released from it — or if I could have forgotten that I had ever been otherwise than as I then was—I could have enjoyed as much happiness in this as in any other situation.

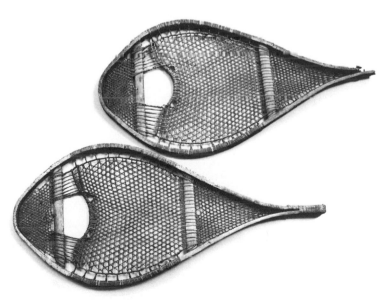

Indian Snowshoes from Michilimackinac. — Courtesy of City of Liverpool Museums

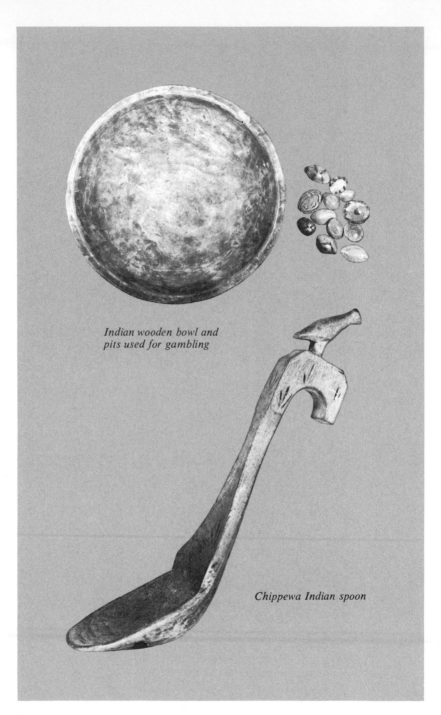

*Indian wooden bowl and
pits used for gambling*

Chippewa Indian spoon

16
LOST

One evening on my return from hunting I found the fire put out and the opening in the top of the lodge covered over with skins, by this means excluding as much as possible external light. I further observed that the ashes were removed from the fireplace, and that dry sand was spread where they had been. Soon after a fire was made without side the cabin in the open air and a kettle hung over it to boil.

I now supposed that a feast was in preparation. I supposed so only; for it would have been indecorous to inquire into the meaning of what I saw. No person among the Indians themselves would use this freedom. Good breeding requires that the spectator should patiently wait the result.

As soon as the darkness of night had arrived the family, including myself, were invited into the lodge. I was now requested not to speak as a feast was about to be given to the dead, whose spirits delight in uninterrupted silence.

As we entered each was presented with his wooden dish and spoon, after receiving which we seated ourselves. The door was next shut, and we remained in perfect darkness.

The master of the family was the master of the feast. Still in the dark he asked every one by turn for his dish and put into each two boiled ears of maize. The whole being served, he began to speak. In his discourse, which lasted half an hour, he called upon the names of his deceased relations and friends, beseeching them to be present to assist him in the chase, and to partake of the food which he had prepared for them. When he had ended, we proceeded to eat our maize, which we did without other noise than what was occasioned by our teeth. The maize was not half boiled, and it took me an hour to consume my share. I was requested not to break the spikes*, as this would be displeasing to the departed spirits of their friends.

When all was eaten Wawatam made another speech, with which the ceremony ended. A new fire was kindled with fresh sparks from flint and steel; and the pipes being smoked, the spikes were carefully buried in a hole made in the ground for that purpose within the lodge. This done, the whole family began to dance, Wawatam singing and beating a drum. The dance continued the greater part of the night, to the great pleasure of the lodge. The night of the feast was that of the first day of November.

On the twentieth of December we took an account of the produce of our hunt and found that we had a hundred beaver skins, as many raccoons, and a large quantity of dried venison; all which was secured from the wolves by being placed upon a scaffold.

A hunting excursion into the interior of the country was resolved on; and early the next morning the bundles were made up by the women for each person to carry. I remarked that the bundle given to me was the lightest, and those carried by the women the largest and heaviest of the whole.

On the first day of our march we advanced about twenty miles and then encamped. Being somewhat fatigued, I could not hunt; but Wawatam killed a stag not far from our encampment. The next morning we moved our lodge to the carcass. At this station we remained two days, employed in drying the meat. The method was to cut it into slices of the thickness of a steak, and then hang it over the fire in the smoke. On the third day we removed and marched till two o'clock in the afternoon.

While the women were busy in erecting and preparing the lodges, I took my gun and strolled away, telling Wawatam that I intended to look out for some fresh meat for supper. He answered that he would do the same; and on this we both left the encampment in different directions.

The sun being visible I entertained no fear of losing my way; but in following several tracks of animals in momentary expectation of falling in with the game I proceeded to a considerable distance, and it was not till near sunset that I thought of returning. The sky, too, had become overcast, and I was therefore left without the sun for my guide. In this situation I walked as fast as I could, always supposing myself to be approaching our encampment, till at length it became so dark that I ran against the trees.

I became convinced that I was lost; and I was alarmed by

---

*The grains of maize called also Indian corn, grow in compact cells round a spike. -Author.

the reflection that I was in a country entirely strange to me, and in danger from strange Indians. With the flint of my gun I made a fire, and then laid me down to sleep. In the night it rained hard. I awoke cold and wet; and as soon as light appeared I recommenced my journey, sometimes walking and sometimes running, unknowing where to go, bewildered, and like a madman.

Toward evening I reached the border of a large lake of which I could scarcely discern the opposite shore. I had never heard of a lake in this part of the country, and therefore felt myself removed further than ever from the object of my pursuit. To tread back my steps appeared to be the most likely means of delivering myself; and I accordingly determined to turn my face directly from the lake, and keep this direction as nearly as I could.

A heavy snow began to descend and night soon afterward came on. On this I stopped and made a fire, and stripping a tree of its sheet of bark, lay down under it to shelter me from the snow. All night at small distances the wolves howled around; and to me seemed to be acquainted with my misfortune.

Amid thoughts the most distracted I was able at length to fall asleep; but it was not long before I awoke, refreshed, and wondering at the terror to which I had yielded myself. That I could really have wanted the means of recovering my way appeared to me almost incredible; and the recollection of it like a dream, or as a circumstance which must have proceeded from the loss of my senses. Had this not happened I could never, as I now thought, have suffered so long without calling to mind the lessons which I had received from my Indian friend for the very purpose of being useful to me in difficulties of this kind. These were that generally speaking the tops of pine trees lean toward the rising of the sun; that moss grows toward the roots of the trees on the side which faces the north; and that the limbs of trees are most numerous and largest on that which faces the south.

Determined to direct my feet by these marks and persuaded that I should thus sooner or later reach Lake Michigan, which I reckoned to be distant about sixty miles, I began my march at break of day. I had not taken, nor wished to take, any nourishment, since I left the encampment; I had with me my gun and ammunition, and was therefore under no anxiety in regard to food. The snow lay about half a foot in depth.

My eyes were now employed upon the trees. When their tops leaned different ways I looked to the moss, or to the branches; and by connecting one with another, I found the means of traveling with some degree of confidence. At four o'clock in the afternoon the sun, to my inexpressible joy, broke from the clouds, and I had now no further need of examining the trees.

In going down the side of a lofty hill I saw a herd of red

deer approaching. Desirous of killing one of them for food, I hid myself in the bushes, and on a large one coming near, presented my piece, which missed fire on account of the priming having been wetted. The animals walked along without taking the least alarm; and having reloaded my gun, I followed them and presented a second time. But now a disaster of the heaviest kind had befallen me; for on attempting to fire I found that I had lost the cock. I had previously lost the screw by which it was fastened to the lock; and to prevent this from being lost also I had tied it in its place with a leather string: the lock, to prevent its catching in the bows, I had carried under my molton coat.

Of all the sufferings which I had experienced this seemed to me the most severe. I was in a strange country, and knew not how far I had to go. I had been three days without food; I was now without the means of procuring myself either food or fire. Despair had almost overpowered me: but I soon resigned myself into the hands of that Providence whose arm had so often saved me, and returned on my track in search of what I had lost. My search was in vain, and I resumed my course, wet, cold and hungry, and almost without clothing.

Bear Claw Necklace

17
The
BEAR
KILLER

The sun was setting fast when I descended a hill at the bottom of which was a small lake entirely frozen over. On drawing near I saw a beaver lodge in the middle offering some faint prospect of food; but I found it already broken up. While I looked at it, it suddenly occurred to me that I had seen it before; and turning my eyes round the place I discovered a small tree which I had myself cut down in the autumn when in company with my friends I had taken the beaver. I was no longer at a loss, but knew both the distance and the route to the encampment. The latter was only to follow the course of a small stream of water which ran from the encampment to the lake on which I stood. An hour before I had thought myself the most miserable of men; and now I leaped for joy and called myself the happiest.

The whole of the night and through all of the succeeding day I walked up the rivulet, and at sunset reached the encampment, where I was received with the warmest expressions of pleasure by the family, by whom I had been given up for lost after a long and vain search for me in the woods.

Some days elapsed, during which I rested myself and recruited my strength: after this I resumed the chase, secure that as the snow had now fallen I could always return by the way I went.

In the course of the month of January I happened to observe that the trunk of a very large pine tree was much torn by the claws of a bear, made both in going up and down. On further examination I saw that there was a large opening in the upper part near which the smaller branches were broken. From these marks and from the additional circumstance that there were no tracks on the snow there was reason to believe that a bear lay concealed in the tree.

On returning to the lodge I communicated my discovery; and it was agreed that all the family should go together in the morning to assist in cutting down the tree, the girth of which was not less than three fathoms. The women at first opposed the undertaking because our axes, being only of a pound and a half weight, were not well adapted to so heavy a labor; but the hope of finding a large bear and obtaining from its fat a great quantity of oil, an article at the time much wanted, at length prevailed.

Accordingly in the morning we surrounded the tree, both men and women, as many at a time as could conveniently work at it; and here we toiled like beaver till the sun went down. This day's work carried us about half way through the trunk; and the next morning we renewed the attack, continuing it till about two o'clock in the afternoon, when the tree fell to the ground. For a few minutes everything remained quiet, and I feared that all our expectations were disappointed; but as I advanced to the opening there came out, to the great satisfaction of all our party, a bear of extraordinary size, which, before she had proceeded many yards, I shot.

The bear being dead, all my assistants approached, and all, but more particularly my old mother (as I was wont to call her), took her head in their hands, stroking and kissing it several times; begging a thousand pardons for taking away her life: calling her their relation and grandmother; and requesting her not to lay the fault upon them, since it was truly an Englishman that had put her to death.

This ceremony was not of long duration; and if it was I that killed their grandmother, they were not themselves behindhand in what remained to be performed. The skin being taken off, we found the fat in several places six inches deep. This being divided into two parts, loaded two persons; and the flesh parts were as much as four persons could carry. In all, the carcass must have exceeded five hundred-weight.

As soon as we reached the lodge the bear's head was adorned with all the trinkets in the possession of the family, such as silver arm bands and wrist bands, and belts of wampum; and then laid upon a scaffold, set up for its reception within the lodge. Near the nose was placed a large quantity of tobacco.

The next morning no sooner appeared than preparations were made for a feast to the manes. The lodge was cleaned and swept; and the head of the bear lifted up, and a new stroud blanket, which had never been used before, spread under it. The pipes were now lit; and Wawatam blew tobacco smoke into the nostrils of the bear, telling me to do the same, and thus appease the anger of the bear on account of my having killed her. I endeavored to persuade my benefactor and friendly adviser that she no longer had any life, and assured him that I was under no apprehension from her displeasure; but the first proposition obtained no credit, and the second gave but little satisfaction.

At length the feast being ready, Wawatam commenced a speech resembling in many things his address to the manes of his relations and departed companions; but having this peculiarity, that he here deplored the necessity under which men labored thus to destroy their *friends*. He represented, however, that the misfortune was unavoidable, since without doing so, they could by no means subsist. The speech ended, we all ate heartily of the bear's flesh; and even the head itself, after remaining three days on the scaffold, was put into the kettle.

It is only the female bear that makes her winter lodging in the upper parts of trees, a practice by which her young are secured from the attacks of wolves and other animals. She brings forth in the winter season; and remains in her lodge till the cubs have gained some strength.

The male always lodges in the ground under the roots of trees. He takes to this habitation as soon as the snow falls, and remains there till it has disappeared. The Indians remark that the bear comes out in the spring with the same fat which he carried in in the autumn; but after exercise of only a few days, becomes lean. Excepting for a short part of the season, the male lives constantly alone.

The fat of our bear was melted down, and the oil filled six porcupine skins.* A part of the meat was cut into strips, and fire dried, after which it was put into the vessels containing the oil, where it remained in perfect preservation until the middle of summer.

February, in the country and by the people where and among whom I was, is called the Moon of Hard or Crusted Snow; for now the snow can bear a man, or at least dogs, in pursuit of animals of the chase. At this season the stag is very successfully hunted, his feet breaking through at every step, and the crust upon the snow cutting his legs with its sharp edges, to the very bone. He is consequently, in this distress, an easy prey; and it frequently happened that we killed twelve in the short space of two hours. By this means we were soon put into possession of four thousand weight of dried venison, which was to be carried on our backs, along with all the rest of our wealth for seventy miles, the distance of our encampment from that part of the lake shore at which in the autumn we left our canoes. This journey it was our next business to perform.

*The animal which, in America, is called a porcupine, is a hedge hog or urchin. -Author.

91

Indian warrior dressed for winter hunting

18
DEATH AMONG
The
INDIANS

Our venison and furs and peltries were to be disposed of at
Michilimackinac, and it was now the season for carrying them to
market. The women therefore prepared our loads; and the morning of departure being come, we set off at daybreak, and continued our march till two o'clock in the afternoon. Where we
stopped we erected a scaffold on which we deposited the bundles
we had brought, and returned to our encampment, which we
reached in the evening. In the morning we carried fresh loads,
which being deposited with the rest, we returned a second time
in the evening. This we repeated till all was forwarded one stage.
Then removing our lodge to the place of deposit, we carried our
goods with the same patient toil a second stage; and so on, till
we were at no great distance from the shores of the lake.

Arrived here, we turned our attention to sugar making, the
management of which, as I have before related, belongs to the
women, the men cutting wood for the fires, and hunting and
fishing. In the midst of this we were joined by several lodges of
Indians, most of whom were of the family to which I belonged,
and had wintered near us. The lands belonged to this family, and
it had therefore the exclusive right to hunt on them. This is
according to the custom of the people; for each family has its
own lands. I was treated very civilly by all the lodges.

Our society had been a short time enlarged by the arrival of
our friends, when an accident occurred which filled all the village
with anxiety and sorrow. A little child belonging to one of our
neighbors fell into a kettle of boiling syrup. It was instantly
snatched out, but with little hope of its recovery.

So long, however, as it lived a continual feast was observed;
and this was made to the Great Spirit and Master of Life, that
he might be pleased to save and heal the child. At this feast I
was a constant guest; and often found difficulty in eating the

large quantity of food, which on such occasions as these is put upon each man's dish. The Indians accustom themselves both to eat much and to fast much, with facility.

Several sacrifices were also offered; among which were dogs, killed and hung upon the tops of poles, with the addition of stroud blankets and other articles. These, also, were given to the Great Spirit in humble hope that he would give efficacy to the medicines employed.

The child died. To preserve the body from the wolves it was placed upon a scaffold, where it remained till we went to the lake, on the border of which was the burial ground of the family.

On our arrival there, which happened in the beginning of April, I did not fail to attend the funeral. The grave was made of a large size, and the whole of the inside lined with birch bark. On the bark was laid the body of the child, accompanied with an axe, a pair of snowshoes, a small kettle, several pairs of common shoes, its own strings of beads, and — because it was a girl — a carrying belt and a paddle. The kettle was filled with meat.

All this was again covered with bark; and at about two feet nearer the surface logs were laid across, and these again covered with bark, so that the earth might by no means fall upon the corpse.

The last act before the burial, performed by the mother crying over the dead body of her child, was that of taking from it a lock of hair for a memorial. While she did this, I endeavored to console her by offering the usual arguments, that the child was happy in being released from the miseries of this present life, and that she should forbear to grieve, because it would be restored to her in another world, happy and everlasting. She answered that she knew it, and that by the lock of hair she should discover her daughter; for she would take it with her. In this she alluded to the day when some pious hand would place in her own grave, along with the carrying-belt and paddle, this little relic, hallowed by maternal tear.

I have frequently inquired into the ideas and opinions of the Indians in regard to futurity, and always found that they were somewhat different in different individuals.

Some suppose their souls to remain in this world, although invisible to human eyes; and capable, themselves, of seeing and hearing their friends, and also of assisting them in moments of distress and danger.

Others dismiss from the mortal scene the unembodied spirit, and send it to a distant world, or country, in which it receives reward or punishment, according to the life which it has led in its prior state. Those who have lived virtuously are transported into a place abounding with every luxury, with deer and all other animals of the woods and water, and where the earth produces, in their greatest perfection, all its sweetest fruits. While, on the other hand, those who have violated or neglected the duties of this life are removed to a barren soil, where they wander up and down among rocks and morasses, and are stung by gnats as large as pigeons.

Otter medicine bag. — Courtesy of City of Liverpool Museums

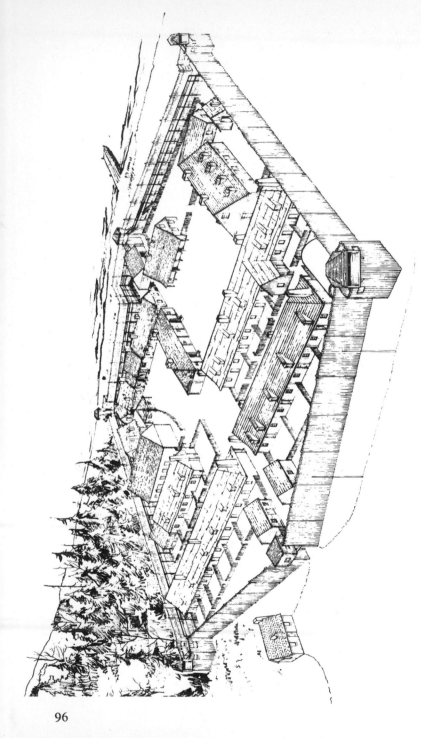

Fort Michilimackinac as it appeared in 1770's. The large barracks facing the parade grounds was constructed in 1769.

19

RETURN *to* MICHILIMACKINAC

While we remained on the border of the lake a watch was kept every night in the apprehension of a speedy attack from the English, who were expected to avenge the massacre of Michilimackinac. The immediate grounds of this apprehension were the constant dreams to this effect of the more aged women. I endeavored to pursuade them that nothing of the kind would take place; but their fears were not to be subdued.

Amid these alarms there came a report concerning a real, though less formidable enemy, discovered in our neighborhood. This was a panther which one of our young men had seen and which animal sometimes attacks and carries away the Indian children. Our camp was immediately on the alert, and we set off into the woods, about twenty in number. We had not proceeded more than a mile before the dogs found the panther, and pursued him to a tree, on which he was shot. He was of a large size.

On the twenty-fifth of April we embarked for Michilimackinac. At La Grande Traverse [Grand Traverse Bay] we met a large party of Indians who appeared to labor, like ourselves, under considerable alarm; and who dared proceed no farther, lest they should be destroyed by the English. Frequent councils of the united bands were held; and interrogations were continually put to myself as to whether or not I knew of any design to attack them. I found that they believed it possible for me to have a foreknowledge of events, and to be informed by dreams of all things doing at a distance.

Protestations of my ignorance were received with but little satisfaction, and incurred the suspicion of a design to conceal my knowledge. On this account therefore, or because I saw them tormented with fears which had nothing but imagination to rest upon, I told them at length that I knew there was no enemy to insult them; and that they might proceed to Michilimackinac

97

without danger from the English. I further, and with more confidence, declared that if ever my countrymen returned to Michilimackinac I would recommend them to their favor on account of the good treatment which I had received from them. Thus encouraged they embarked at an early hour the next morning. In crossing the bay we experienced a storm of thunder and lightning.

Our port was the village of L'Arbre Croche, which we reached in safety, and where we stayed till the following day. At this village we found several persons who had been lately at Michilimackinac, and from them we had the satisfaction of learning that all was quiet there. The remainder of our voyage was therefore performed with confidence.

In the evening of the twenty-seventh we landed at the fort, which now contained only two French traders. The Indians who had arrived before us were very few in number; and by all who were of our party I was used very kindly. I had the entire freedom both of the fort and camp.

Wawatam and myself settled our stock and paid our debts; and this done, I found that my share of what was left consisted in a hundred beaver skins, sixty raccoon skins, and six otter, of the total value of about one hundred and sixty dollars. With these earnings of my winter's toil I proposed to purchase some clothes of which I was much in need, having been six months without a shirt; but on inquiring into the prices of goods I found that all my funds would not go far. I was able, however, to buy two shirts at ten pounds of beaver each; a pair of *leggings*, or pantaloons, of scarlet cloth, which with the ribbon to garnish them *fashionably*, cost me fifteen pounds of beaver; a blanket, at twenty pounds of beaver; and some other articles at proportionable rates. In this manner my wealth was soon reduced; but not before I had laid in a good stock of ammunition and tobacco. To the use of the latter I had become much attached during the winter. It was my principal recreation after returning from the chase; for my companions in the lodge were unaccustomed to pass the time in conversation. Among the Indians the topics of conversation are but few, and limited for the most part to the transactions of the day, the number of animals which they have killed, and of those which have escaped their pursuit; and other incidents of the chase. Indeed, the causes of taciturnity among the Indians may be easily understood if we consider how many occasions of speech, which present themselves to us, are utterly unknown to them; the records of history, the pursuits of science, the disquisitions of philosophy, the systems of politics, the business and the amusements of the day, and the transactions of the four corners of the world.

Eight days had passed in tranquillity when there arrived a band of Indians from the Bay of Saguenaum [Saginaw Bay]. They had assisted at the siege of Detroit, and came to muster as many recruits for that service as they could. For my own part, I was soon informed that as I was the only Englishman in the place they proposed to kill me in order to give their friends a mess of English broth to raise their courage.

This intelligence was not of the most agreeable kind; and in consequence of receiving it, I requested my friend to carry me to the Sault de Ste. Marie, at which place I knew the Indians to be peaceably inclined, and that M. Cadotte enjoyed a powerful influence over their conduct. They considered M. Cadotte as their chief; and he was not only my friend, but a friend to the English. It was by him that the Chippewa of Lake Superior were prevented from joining Pontiac.

Wawatam was not slow to exert himself for my preservation; but, leaving Michilimackinac in the night, transported myself and all his lodge to Point St. Ignace, on the opposite side of the strait. Here we remained till daylight, and then went into the Bay of Boutchitaouy, in which we spend three days in fishing and hunting, and where we found plenty of wild fowl. Leaving the bay we made for the Isle aux Outardes, where we were obliged to put in on account of the wind's coming ahead. We proposed sailing for the Sault the next morning.

But when the morning came Wawatam's wife complained that she was sick, adding that she had had bad dreams, and knew that if we went to the Sault we should all be destroyed. To have argued at this time against the infallibility of dreams would have been extremely inadvisable, since I should have appeared to be guilty, not only of an odious want of faith but also of a still more odious want of sensibility to the possible calamities of a family which had done so much for the alleviation of mine. I was silent; but the disappointment seemed to seal my fate. No prospect opened to console me. To return to Michilimackinac could only ensure my destruction; and to remain at the island was to brave almost equal danger, since it lay in the direct route between the fort and the Missisaki, along which the Indians from Detroit were hourly expected to pass on the business of their mission. I doubted not but, taking advantage of the solitary situation of the family, they would carry into execution their design of killing me.

Archaeology dig at Fort Michilimackinac. Over 200 building foundations, trash deposits, and basements, as well as more than 400,000 artifacts from the 18th century have been found.

20
FLIGHT
to
SAULT SAINTE MARIE

Unable, therefore, to take any part in the direction of our course, but a prey at the same time to the most anxious thoughts as to my own condition, I passed all the day on the highest part, to which I could climb, of a tall tree, and whence the lake on both sides of the island lay open to my view. Here I might hope to learn at the earliest possible moment the approach of canoes, and by this means be warned in time to conceal myself.

On the second morning I returned as soon as it was light to my watch-tower, on which I had not been long before I discovered a sail coming from Michilimackinac.

The sail was a white one, and much larger than those usually employed by the northern Indians. I therefore indulged a hope that it might be a Canadian canoe, on its voyage to Montreal; and that I might be able to prevail upon the crew to take me with them and thus release me from all my troubles.

My hopes continued to gain strength; for I soon persuaded myself that the manner in which the paddles were used on board the canoe was Canadian, and not Indian. My spirits were elated; but disappointment had become so usual with me that I could not suffer myself to look to the event with any strength of confidence.

Enough, however, appeared at length to demonstrate itself to induce me to descend the tree and repair to the lodge, with my tidings and schemes of liberty. The family congratulated me on the approach of so fair an opportunity of escape; and my father and brother (for he was alternately each of these) lit his pipe and presented it to me saying, "My son, this may be the last time that ever you and I shall smoke out of the same pipe. I am sorry to part with you. You know the affection which I always have borne you, and the dangers to which I have exposed myself and family to preserve you from your enemies; and I am happy to find that my efforts promise not to have been in vain." At this time a boy came into the lodge, informing us that the canoe had come from Michilimackinac and was bound to the Sault de Ste. Marie. It was manned by three Canadians, and was carrying home Madame Cadotte, the wife of M. Cadotte already mentioned.

My hopes of going to Montreal being now dissipated, I resolved on accompanying Madame Cadotte, with her permission, to the Sault. On communicating my wishes to Madame Cadotte, she cheerfully acceded to them. Madame Cadotte, as I have already mentioned, was an Indian woman of the Chippewa nation; and she was very generally respected.

My departure fixed upon, I returned to the lodge, where I packed up my wardrobe, consisting of my two shirts, pair of *leggings*, and blanket. Besides these I took a gun and ammunition, presenting what remained further to my host. I also returned the silver armbands with which the family had decorated me the year before.

We now exchanged farewells, with an emotion entirely reciprocal. I did not quit the lodge without the most grateful sense of the many acts of goodness which I had experienced in it, nor without the sincerest respect for the virtues which I had witnessed among its members. All the family accompanied me to the beach; and the canoe had no sooner put off, than Wawatam commenced an address to the Kichi Manito, beseeching him to take care of me, his brother, till we should next meet. This, he had told me, would not be long, as he intended to return to Michilimackinac for a short time only, and would then follow me to the Sault. We had proceeded too great a distance to allow of our hearing his voice, before Wawatam had ceased to offer up his prayers.

Being now no longer in the society of Indians I laid aside the dress, putting on that of a Canadian; a molton, or blanket coat, over my shirt, and a handkerchief about my head, hats being very little worn in this country.

At daybreak on the second morning of our voyage we embarked, and presently perceived several canoes behind us. As they approached, we ascertained them to be the fleet bound for the Missisaki, of which I had been so long in dread. It amounted to twenty sail.

On coming up with us and surrounding our canoe, and amid general inquiries concerning the news, an Indian challenged me for an Englishman and his companions supported him by declaring that I looked very like one; but I affected not to understand any of the questions which they asked me, and Madame Cadotte assured them that I was a Canadian whom she had brought on his first voyage from Montreal.

The following day saw us safely landed at the Sault, where I experienced a generous welcome from M. Cadotte. There were thirty warriors at this place, restrained from joining in the war only by M. Cadotte's influence.

Here for five days I was once more in possession of tranquillity; but on the sixth a young Indian came into M. Cadotte's saying that a canoe full of warriors had just arrived from Michilimackinac; that they had inquired for me; and that he believed their intentions to be bad. Nearly at the same time a message came from the good chief of the village desiring me to conceal myself until he should discover the views and temper of the strangers.

A garret was a second time my place of refuge; and it was not long before the Indians came to M. Cadotte's. My friend immediately informed Mutchikiwish,* their chief, who was related to his wife, of the design imputed to them of mischief against myself. Mutchikiwish frankly acknowledged that they had had such a design; but added that if displeasing to M. Cadotte, it should be abandoned. He then further stated that their errand was to raise a party of warriors to return with them to Detroit; and that it had been their intention to take me with them.

In regard to the principal of the two objects thus disclosed M. Cadotte proceeded to assemble all the chiefs and warriors of the village; and these, after deliberating for some time among themselves, sent for the strangers, to whom both M. Cadotte and the chief of the village addressed a speech. In these speeches, after recurring to the designs confessed to have been entertained against myself, who was now declared to be under the immediate protection of all the chiefs, by whom any insult I might sustain would be avenged, the ambassadors were peremptorily told that they might go back as they came, none of the young men of this village being foolish enough to join them.

A moment after, a report was brought that a canoe had just arrived from Niagara. As this was a place from which everyone was anxious to hear news, a message was sent to these fresh strangers requesting them to come to the council.

The strangers came accordingly, and being seated, a long silence ensued. At length one of them, taking up a belt of wampum, addressed himself thus to the assembly: "My friends and brothers, I am come, with this belt, from our great father, Sir William Johnson [Superintendent of Indian Affairs in the Northern Department]. He desired me to come to you as his ambassador, and tell you that he is making a great feast at

---

*Mutchikiwish, or Matchekewis, led the Chippewas who attacked the garrison at Michilimackinac on June 2, 1763. - Editor.

Fort Niagara; that his kettles are all ready, and his fires lit. He invites you to partake of the feast, in common with your friends, the Six Nations, which have all made peace with the English. He advises you to seize this opportunity of doing the same, as you cannot otherwise fail of being destroyed; for the English are on their march with a great army, which will be joined by different nations of Indians. In a word, before the fall of the leaf they will be at Michilimackinac, and the Six Nations [of the Iroquois] with them."

The tenor of this speech greatly alarmed the Indians of the Sault, who after a very short consultation agreed to send twenty deputies to Sir William Johnson at Niagara. This was a project highly interesting to me, since it offered me the means of leaving the country. I intimated this to the chief of the village, and received his promise that I should accompany the deputation.

Very little time was proposed to be lost in setting forward on the voyage; but the occasion was of too much magnitude not to call for more than human knowledge and discretion; and preparations were accordingly made for solemnly invoking and consulting the GREAT TURTLE, [the chief guardian spirit of the Chippewa].

Chippewa moccasins. — Courtesy of City of Liverpool Museums

21
CONSULTING
the
GREAT TURTLE

For invoking and consulting the Great Turtle the first thing to be done was the building of a large house or wigwam, within which was placed a species of tent for the use of the priest and reception of the spirit. The tent was formed of moose-skins, hung over a framework of wood. Five poles, or rather pillars, of five different species of timber, about ten feet in height and eight inches in diameter were set in a circle of about four feet in diameter. The holes made to receive them were about two feet deep; and the pillars being set, the holes were filled up again, with the earth which had been dug out. At top the pillars were bound together by a circular hoop, or girder. Over the whole of this edifice were spread the moose-skins, covering it at top and round the sides, and made fast with thongs of the same; except that on one side a part was left unfastened, to admit of the entrance of the priest.

The ceremonies did not commence but with the approach of night. To give light within the house several fires were kindled round the tent. Nearly the whole village assembled in the house, and myself among the rest. It was not long before the priest appeared almost in a state of nakedness. As he approached the tent the skins were lifted up as much as was necessary to allow of his creeping under them on his hands and knees. His head was scarcely within side when the edifice, massy as it has been described, began to shake; and the skins were no sooner let fall than the sounds of numerous voices were heard beneath them, some yelling, some barking as dogs, some howling like wolves; and in this horrible concert were mingled screams and sobs, as of despair, anguish, and the sharpest pain. Articulate speech was also uttered, as if from human lips; but in a tongue unknown to any of the audience.

After some time these confused and frightful noises were succeeded by a perfect silence; and now a voice not heard before
seemed to manifest the arrival of a new character in the tent.
This was a low and feeble voice, resembling the cry of a young
puppy. The sound was no sooner distinguished, than all the
Indians clapped their hands for joy, exclaiming that this was the
Chief Spirit, the TURTLE, the spirit that never lied. Other voices
which they had discriminated from time to time they had previously hissed, as recognizing them to belong to evil and lying
spirits, which deceive mankind.

New sounds came from the tent. During the space of half
an hour, a succession of songs were heard, in which a diversity
of voices met the ear. From his first entrance till these songs
were finished we heard nothing in the proper voice of the priest;
but now he addressed the multitude, declaring the presence of
the GREAT TURTLE and the spirit's readiness to answer such
questions as should be proposed.

The questions were to come from the chief of the village,
who was silent, however, till after he had put a large quantity
of tobacco into the tent, introducing it at the aperture. This was
a sacrifice, offered to the spirit; for spirits are supposed by the
Indians to be as fond of tobacco as themselves. The tobacco accepted, he desired the priest to inquire whether or not the English
were preparing to make war upon the Indians? and whether or
not there were at Fort Niagara a large number of English troops?

These questions having been put by the priest, the tent instantly shook; and for some seconds after it continued to rock so
violently that I expected to see it levelled with the ground. All
this was a prelude, as I supposed, to the answers to be given;
but a terrific cry announced, with sufficient intelligibility, the departure of the TURTLE.

A quarter of an hour elapsed in silence, and I waited impatiently to discover what was to be the next incident in this
scene of imposture. It consisted in the return of the spirit, whose
voice was again heard, and who now delivered a continued
speech. The language of the GREAT TURTLE, like that which
we had heard before, was wholly unintelligible to every ear, that
of his priest excepted; and it was, therefore, that not till the
latter gave us an interpretation, which did not commence before
the spirit had finished, that we learned the purport of this extraordinary communication.

The spirit, as we were now informed by the priest, had during his short absence crossed Lake Huron and even proceeded as
far as Fort Niagara, which is at the head of Lake Ontario, and
thence to Montreal. At Fort Niagara he had seen no great number of soldiers; but on descending the St. Lawrence as low as

106

Montreal, he had found the river covered with boats and the boats filled with soldiers, in number like the leaves of the trees. He had met them on their way up the river, coming to make war upon the Indians.

The chief had a third question to propose, and the spirit, without a fresh journey to Fort Niagara, was able to give it an instant and most favorable answer: "If," said the chief, "the Indians visit Sir William Johnson, will they be received as friends?"

"Sir William Johnson," said the spirit (and after the spirit, the priest) "Sir William Johnson will fill their canoes with presents; with blankets, kettles, guns, gunpowder and shot, and large barrels of rum such as the stoutest of the Indians will not be able to lift; and every man will return in safety to his family."

At this the transport was universal; and amid the clapping of hands, a hundred voices exclaimed, "I will go, too. I will go, too."

The question of public interest being resolved, individuals were now permitted to seize the opportunity of inquiring into the condition of their absent friends, and the fate of such as were sick. I observed that the answers given to these questions allowed of much latitude of interpretation.

Amid this general inquisitiveness I yielded to the solicitations of my own anxiety for the future, and having first, like the rest, made by offering of tobacco, I inquired, whether or not I should ever revisit my native country. The question being put by the priest, the tent shook as usual; after which I received this answer: That I should take courage and fear no danger, for that nothing would happen to hurt me; and that I should in the end reach my friends and country in safety. These assurances wrought so strongly on my gratitude that I presented an additional and extra offering of tobacco.

The GREAT TURTLE continued to be consulted till nearly midnight, when all the crowd dispersed to their respective lodges. I was on the watch through the scene I have described to detect the particular contrivances by which the fraud was carried on; but such was the skill displayed in the performance, or such my deficiency of penetration, that I made no discoveries, but came away as I went, with no more than those general surmises which will naturally be entertained by every reader.

(M. de Champlain has left an account of an exhibition of the nature here described, which may be seen in Charlevoix's Histoire et Description Generale de la Nouvelle France, *Livre IV. This took place in the year 1609, and was performed among a party of warriors composed of Algonquin, Montagnez, and Hurons. Carver witnessed another among the Cristinaux. In each case the details are somewhat different, but the outline is the same. M. de Champlain mentions that he saw the jongleur shake the stakes or pillars*

of the tent. I was not so fortunate; but this is the obvious explanation of that part of the mystery to which it refers. Captain Carver leaves the whole in darkness. -Author.)

On the tenth of June I embarked with the Indian deputation, composed of sixteen men. Twenty had been the number originally designed; and upwards of fifty actually engaged themselves to the council for the undertaking, to say nothing of the general enthusiasm at the moment of hearing the GREAT TURTLE'S promises. But exclusively of the degree of timidity which still prevailed, we are to take into account the various domestic calls, which might supersede all others, and detain many with their families.

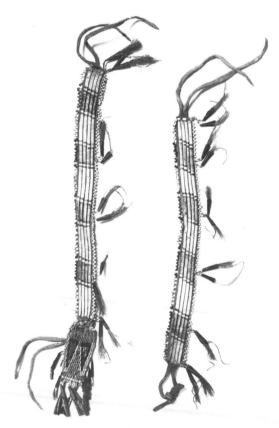

Indian garters decorated with tinkling cones, trade beads and porcupine quills. — Courtesy of City of Liverpool Museums

22
From the
SAULT *to*
FORT NIAGARA

In the evening of the second day of our voyage we reached the mouth of the Missisaki, where we found about forty Indians, by whom we were received with abundant kindness, and at night regaled at a great feast, held on account of our arrival. The viand was a preparation of the roe of the sturgeon, beat up and boiled, and of the consistence of porridge.

After eating, several speeches were made to us, of which the general topic was a request that we should recommend the village to Sir William Johnson. This request was also specially addressed to me, and I promised to comply with it.

On the fourteenth of June we passed the village of La Cloche, of which the greater part of the inhabitants were absent, being already on a visit to Sir William Johnson. This circumstance greatly encouraged the companions of my voyage, who now saw that they were not the first to run into danger.

The next day about noon, the wind blowing very hard, we were obliged to put ashore at Point aux Grondines, a place of which some description had been given above [page 17]. While the Indians erected a hut, I employed myself in making a fire. As I was gathering wood, an unusual sound fixed my attention for a moment; but as it presently ceased, and as I saw nothing from which I could suppose it to proceed, I continued my employment, till, advancing farther, I was alarmed by a repetition. I imagined that it came from above my head; but after looking that way in vain, I cast my eyes on the ground and there discovered a rattle-snake, at not more than two feet from my naked legs. The reptile was coiled, and its head raised considerably above its body. Had I advanced another step before my discovery I must have trodden upon it.

I no sooner saw the snake than I hastened to the canoe, in order to procure my gun; but the Indians, observing what I was doing, inquired the occasion, and being informed, begged me to desist. At the same time they followed me to the spot, with their pipes and tobacco-pouches in their hands. On returning, I found the snake still coiled.

The Indians on their part surrounded it, all addressing it by turns, and calling it their *grandfather*; but yet keeping at some distance. During this part of the ceremony they filled their pipes; and now each blew the smoke toward the snake, who, as it appeared to me, really received it with pleasure. In a word, after remaining coiled and receiving incense for the space of half an hour, it stretched itself along the ground in visible good humor. Its length was between four and five feet. Having remained outstretched for some time, at last it moved slowly away, the Indians following it and still addressing it by the title of grandfather, beseeching it to take care of their families during their absence, and to be pleased to open the heart of Sir William Johnson so that he might show them charity and fill their canoe with rum.

One of the chiefs added a petition that the snake would take no notice of the insult which had been offered him by the Englishman, who would even have put him to death but for the interference of the Indians, to whom it was hoped he would impute no part of the offense. They further requested that he would remain and inhabit their country, and not return among the English; that is, go eastward.

After the rattlesnake was gone, I learned that this was the first time that an individual of the species had been seen so far to the northward and westward of the River Des Francais, a circumstance, moreover, from which my companions were disposed to infer that this *manito* had come, or been sent, on purpose to meet them; that his errand had been no other than to stop them on their way; and that consequently it would be most advisable to return to the point of departure. I was so fortunate, however, as to prevail with them to embark, and at six o'clock in the evening we again encamped. Very little was spoken of through the evening, the rattlesnake excepted.

Early the next morning we proceeded. We had a serene sky and very little wind, and the Indians, therefore, determined on steering across the lake to an island which just appeared in the horizon; saving, by this course, a distance of thirty miles, which would be lost in keeping the shore. At nine o'clock, A. M., we had a light breeze astern, to enjoy the benefit of which we hoisted sail. Soon after the wind increased and the Indians, beginning to be alarmed, frequently called on the rattlesnake to come to their assistance. By degrees the waves grew high; and at eleven o'clock it blew a hurricane and we expected every moment to be swallowed up. From prayers the Indians now proceeded to sacrifices, both alike offered to the god-rattlesnake, or *manito-kinibic*. One of the chiefs took a dog, and after tying its fore-legs together threw it overboard, at the same time calling on the snake to preserve us from being drowned, and desiring him to satisfy his hunger with the carcass of the dog. The snake was unpropitious, and the wind increased. Another chief sacrificed another dog, with the addition of some tobacco. In the prayer which accompanied these gifts he besought the snake, as before, not to avenge upon the Indians the insult which he had received from myself, in the conception of a design to put him to death. He assured the snake that I was absolutely an Englishman, and of kin neither to him nor to them.

At the conclusion of this speech an Indian, who sat near me, observed that if we were drowned it would be for my fault alone, and that I ought myself to be sacrificed to appease the angry manito; nor was I without apprehensions that in case of extremity this would be my fate; but happily for me the storm at length abated, and we reached the island safely.

The next day was calm and we arrived at the entrance* of the navigation which leads to Lake aux Claies. *(This lake, which is now called Lake Simcoe, lies between Lakes Huron and Ontario. -Author.)* We presently passed two short carrying-places, at each of which were several lodges of Indians,** containing only women and children, the men being gone to the council at Niagara. From this, as from a former instance, my companions derived new courage.

On the eighteenth of June we crossed Lake aux Claies, which appeared to be upward of twenty miles in length. At its further end we came to the carrying-place of Toranto. *(Toranto, or Toronto, is the name of a French trading house on Lake Ontario, built near the site of the present town of York, the capital of the province of Upper Canada. -Author.)* Here the Indians obliged me to carry a burden of more than a hundred pounds weight. The day was very hot and the woods and marshes abounded with mosquitoes; but the Indians walked at a quick pace, and I could by no means see myself left behind. The whole country was a thick forest, through which our only road was a footpath, or such as in America is exclusively termed an *Indian path*.

Next morning at ten o'clock we reached the shore of Lake Ontario. Here we were employed two days in making canoes out of the bark of the elm tree in which we were to transport our-selves to Niagara. For this purpose the Indians first cut down a

---

*This is the Bay of Matchedash, or Matchitashk. -Author.

**These Indians are called Chippewas, of the particular description called Missisakies; and from their residence at Matchedash, or Matchitashk, also called Matchedash or Matkitashk Indians. -Author.

111

tree; then stripped off the bark in one entire sheet of about eighteen feet in length, the incision being lengthwise. The canoe was now complete as to its top, bottom, and sides. Its ends were next closed by sewing the bark together; and a few ribs and bars being introduced, the architecture was finished. In this manner we made two canoes, of which one carried eight men and the other nine.

On the twenty-first we embarked at Toranto and encamped, in the evening, four miles short of Fort Niagara, which the Indians would not approach till morning.

At dawn the Indians were awake, and presently assembled in council, still doubtful as to the fate they were to encounter. I assured them of the most friendly welcome; and at length, after painting themselves with the most lively colors in token of their own peaceable views, and after singing the song which is in use among them on going into danger, they embarked and made for Point Missisaki, which is on the north side of the mouth of the river or strait of Niagara, as the fort is on the south. A few minutes after, I crossed over to the fort; and here I was received by Sir William Johnson in a manner for which I have ever been gratefully attached to his person and memory.

Thus was completed my escape from the sufferings and dangers which the capture of Fort Michilimackinac brought upon me; but the property which I had carried into the Upper Country was left behind. The reader will, therefore, be far from attributing to me any idle or unaccountable motive when he finds me returning to the scene of my misfortune.

Wampum belt of white and purple shell beads. — Courtesy of City of Liverpool Museums

23
MICHILIMACKINAC REGAINED

At Fort Niagara I found General [John] Bradstreet with a force of three thousand men, preparing to embark for Detroit with a view to raise the siege which it had sustained against Pontiac, for twelve months together. The English in this time had lost many men; and Pontiac had been frequently on the point of carrying the place, though gallantly defended by Major [Henry] Gladwyn, its commandant.

General Bradstreet, having learned my history, informed me that it was his design, on arriving at Detroit, to detach a body of troops to Michilimackinac, and politely assured me of his services in recovering my property there. With these temptations before me I was easily induced to follow the General to Detroit.

But I was not to go as a mere looker-on. On the contrary, I was invested with the honor of a command in a corps, of the exploits, however, of which I can give no flattering account.

Besides the sixteen Saulteurs, or Chippewa, of the Sault de Ste. Marie, with whom I had come to Fort Niagara, there were already at that place eighty Matchedash Indians, the same whose lodges we passed at the carrying-places of Lake aux Claies. These ninety-six men being formed into what was called the Indian Battalion, were furnished with necessaries, and I was appointed to be their leader — me, whose best hope it had very lately been to live through their forbearance.

On the tenth of July the army marched for Fort Schlausser, a stockaded post above the Great Falls, [Niagara Falls] and I ordered my Indians to march also. Only ten of the whole number were ready at the call, but the rest promised to follow the next morning. With my skeleton battalion, therefore, I proceeded to the fort, and there waited the whole of the next day, impatiently expecting the remainder. I waited in vain; and the day following returned to Fort Niagara, when I found that they had all deserted,

Private
BRITISH 60th FOOT ROYAL AMERICANS

going back to their homes, equipment and all, by the way of Toranto. I thought their conduct, though dishonest, not very extraordinary; since the Indians employed in the siege of Detroit, against whom we were leading them, were at peace with their nation, and their own friends and kinsmen. Amid the general desertion four Missisakies joined the ten whom I had left at Fort Schlausser.

For the transport of the army on Lake Erie barges had been expressly built, capable of carrying a hundred men each, with their provisions. One of these was allowed to me and my Indians.

On the fourteenth we embarked at Fort Schlausser, and in the evening encamped at Fort Erie. Here the Indians, growing drunk, amused themselves with a disorderly firing of their muskets in the camp. On this, General Bradstreet ordered all the rum in the Indian quarters to be seized and thrown away. The Indians, in consequence, threatened to desert; and the general, judging it proper to assume a high tone, immediately assembled the chiefs (for among the fourteen Indians there were more chiefs than one) and told them that he had no further occasion for their services, and that such of them as should follow his camp would be considered as soldiers, and subjected to military discipline accordingly. After hearing the General's speech, the majority set out for Fort Niagara the same evening, and thence returned to their own country by the way of Toranto; and thus was my poor battalion still further diminished.

On our fifth day from Fort Schlausser we reached Presqu'isle, [Eric, Pennsylvania] where we dragged our barges over the neck of land, but not without straining their timbers; and with more loss of time, as I believe, than if we had rowed round. On the twentieth day we were off the mouth of the river which falls into Sandusky Bay, where a council of war was held on the question whether it were more advisable to attack and destroy the Indian villages on the Miami or to proceed for Detroit direct. Early the next morning, it having been determined that, considering the villages were populous as well as hostile, it was necessary to destroy them, we entered the Miami; but were presently met by a deputation offering peace. The offer was accepted; but it was not till after two days, during which we had begun to be doubtful of the enemy's intention, that the chiefs arrived. When they came, a sort of armistice was agreed upon,* and they promised to meet the General at Detroit within fifteen days. At that place terms of peace were to be settled in a general council. On the eighth of August we landed at Detroit.

---

*Despite their promise of peace the Indians continued attacking the frontier. -Editor.

The Indians of the Miami were punctual, and a general peace was concluded. Pontiac, who could do nothing against the force which was now opposed to him and who saw himself abandoned by his followers, unwilling to trust his fortunes with the English, fled to the Illinois.*

On the day following that of the treaty of peace, Captain Howard was detached, with two companies and three hundred Canadian volunteers, for Fort Michilimackinac, and I embarked at the same time.

From Detroit to the mouth of Lake Huron is called a distance of eighty miles. From the fort to Lake St. Claire, which is only seven miles, the lands are cultivated on both sides of the strait, and appeared to be laid out in very comfortable farms. In the strait, on the right hand is a village of Huron, and at the mouth of Lake St. Claire a village of Ottawa. We met not a single Indian on our voyage, the report of the arrival of the English army having driven every one from the shores of the lake.

On our arrival at Michilimackinac the Ottawa of L'Arbre Croche were sent for to the fort. They obeyed the summons, bringing with them some Chippewa chiefs, and peace was concluded with both.

For myself, having much property due to me at Ste. Marie's, I resolved on spending the winter at that place. I was in part successful; and in the spring I returned to Michilimackinac.

The pause which I shall here make in my narrative might with some propriety have been placed at the conclusion of the preceding chapter; but it is here that my first series of adventures are brought truly to an end. What remains belongs to a second enterprise, wholly independent of the preceding.

---

*It is very possible, nevertheless, that Pontiac subsequently joined the English, and that a portion of what is related by Carver, concerning his latter history and death, is true. It cannot, however, be intended to insinuate that an English governor was party to the assassination:

"Pontiac henceforward seemed to have aside the animosity he had hitherto born towards the English, and apparently became their zealous friend. To reward this new attachment, and to insure a continuance of it, government allowed him a handsome pension. But his restless and intriguing spirit would not suffer him to be grateful for this allowance, and his conduct at length grew suspicious; so that going, in the year 1767, to hold a council in the country of the Illinois, a faithful Indian, who was either commissioned by one of the English governors, or instigated by the love he bore the English nation, attended him as a spy; and being convinced from the speech Pontiac made in the council, that he still retained his former prejudices against those for whom he now professed a friendship, he plunged his knife into his heart, as soon as he had done speaking, and laid him dead on the spot." -Author.

*Pontiac lapsed into obscurity and in 1769 was murdered by a Peoria Indian while walking in the village of Cahokia, Illinois. -Editor.

British traders, such as Alexander Henry, brought their English culture to Fort Michilimackinac. All items found by archaeologists on the site.

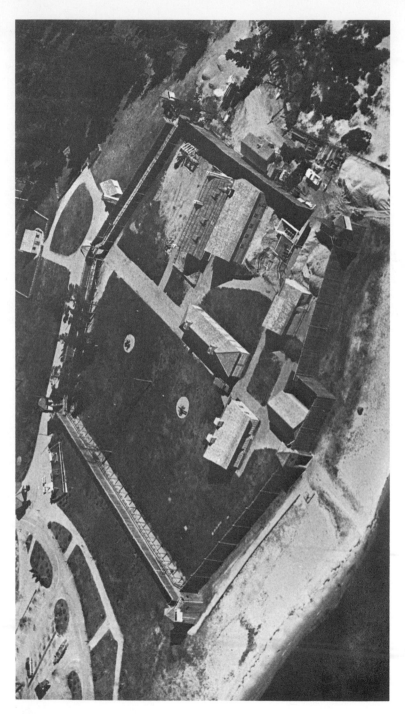

Aerial view of reconstructed fort

AFTERWARD

Having returned to Michilimackinac in the Spring of 1765 Alexander Henry set about rebuilding his fortune. The commandant of Fort Michilimackinac, Captain William Howard, granted him a monopoly of trade on Lake Superior and Henry purchased on credit four canoe loads of merchandise valued at ten thousand pounds of beaver. Engaging twelve canoemen and provisioning them with fifty bushels of corn, Henry and his men embarked for Sault Saint Marie on July 14, 1765. For the next eleven years Henry's interest was focused on Lake Superior and beyond. Returning occasionally to Michilimackinac to outfit his canoes with new merchandise and provisions, Henry devoted most of his time to trading with the distant tribes — some as far away as the Canadian Great Plains and the trading posts of the Hudson's Bay Company. Spurred on by a restless curiosity, as well as the desire for gain, Henry observed with an intense fascination the novel customs of each new tribe he encountered.

While trading along the southern shore of Lake Superior, Henry was attracted by natural outcroppings of rich veins of copper ore and was instrumental in forming a company with an Englishman Alexander Baxter and the fur trader Henry Bostwick to exploit them. Hundreds of pounds sterling were expended to extract and export the ore, but the costs proved prohibitive and by 1774 the company was defunct.

After spending the early months of 1776 tramping on snowshoes far out on the rolling plains of Saskatchewan, Henry decided to give up the life of an active fur trader which he had been pursuing for the past fifteen years. Leaving the upper Lakes region Henry returned to Montreal in October, 1776, to be confronted with the ominous turmoils of the American Revolution, which had thus far had few repercussions among the interior tribes.

We know a great deal about Alexander Henry prior to October, 1776, when Part Two of his *Travels and Adventures* concludes the narrative. From 1776 until his death in 1824 we know far less.

During the American Revolution, Henry made several voyages to England and to Europe and on one occasion was introduced to the beautiful yet tragic Queen of France, Marie Antoinette. Returning to Montreal, Henry operated as a wholesale fur trader, sending his hired clerks into the interior and utilizing the many contacts with such men as Peter Pond, John Askin, Henry Bostwick, and Benjamin and Joseph Frobisher whom he had come to know during his years in the wilderness. Henry, himself, made several trips to Michilimackinac and the upper Lakes country to tend to his affairs. Success alternated with failure, and he made and lost several fortunes before he retired from the fur trade in 1796 and devoted his talents to a general merchandising business. Henry, however, fostered fond memories of his adventurous past and finally commited some of them to paper in 1809 from the notes which he had accumulated during those exciting years. Henry remained vigorous and active until the end of his eighty-five years. After adventures and hair-breadth escapes too numerous to mention, he died placidly in his own bed, a victim of the inevitable forces of old age rather than the scalping knife of a Chippewa.

Long before Henry's death in 1824, Fort Michilimackinac, which had been the scene of his most remembered adventures, had ceased to exist. When the British, frightened by the threat of an American naval attack, moved their garrison to a new and stronger location at Mackinac Island in 1781, the traders, needing protection, followed. Their homes and warehouses, stripped of all items of value, succumbed to the elements and decay. Roofs caved in, palisades toppled and leaves and sand obliterated the remains of man at Michilimackinac.

The fort and the village around it lay virtually undisturbed until 1959 when an archaelogical team began to search for the remnants of the nearly forgotten metropolis. Year by year in an orderly and laborious manner the soil of Michilimackinac was sifted, artifacts recovered, and building foundations delineated. This data, coupled with that retrieved from maps, letters and business records dating from Alexander Henry's period, were combined to make it possible once again to reconstruct the Fort and town which Henry had known. Now, over two hundred years after Henry hid in a Michilimackinac garret, the fort and town are being rebuilt as he knew them. The economic reason of the Fort's earlier existence, the fur trade, no longer is operative, but the desire of contemporary Americans to understand the stirring events of the past has made the current reconstruction possible.

One can once again stand on the site of the Chippewa ball game and enter the open gate through which the painted savages rushed. One also can see the beads, guns, axes, and kettles which excited the Indians' lust. Now, standing within the lofty palisades of Fort Michilimackinac with a copy of Alexander Henry's account in his hand, it is possible for the visitor to take a long step back in time and relive for himself the adventures of the man whom the Indians called "the handsome Englishman."

British military uniform buttons found at Michilimackinac. On left is 60th or Royal American button of unit stationed at the fort during the attack of 1763.

Eighteenth century letter seal that Alexander Henry may have used. Found by archaeologists on the site.

Spanish "piece of eight" and English half-penny were common coins at the fort in 1760's.

INDEX

7

Chippewa moccasin. — Courtesy of City of Liverpool Museums

The Editor

Dr. David A. Armour received his Ph.D. in Colonial American History from Northwestern University, Evanston, Illinois in 1965. After teaching for several years as Assistant Professor of Colonial American History at the University of Wisconsin - Milwaukee, he was appointed in 1967 Assistant Director of the Mackinac Island Park Commission. He is also editor of *Historical Archaeology*, the annual publication of the Society for Historical Archaeology.

Michilimackinac restored

LAKE SUPERIOR

THESSALON RIVER

MISSISSAKI RIVER

LAKE NIPISSING

SAULT STE. MARIE

1764
1762

1764

1761

FRE
RI

MICHILIMACKINAC

BEAVER ISLANDS

L'ARBRE CROCHE

1763-1764

LAKE HURON

AUX SABLES RIVER

SAGINAW BAY

1764

LAKE MICHIGAN

GREEN BAY

DETROIT

FORT ST. JOSEPH

LAKE ERIE

PRES
IS

SANDUSKY